VOICES *from the* RUST BELT

VOICES *from the* RUST BELT

Edited by

ANNE TRUBEK

PICADOR

NEW YORK

picadorusa.com • instagram.com/picador
twitter.com/picadorusa • facebook.com/picadorusa

Designed by Steven Seighman

Picador® is a U.S. registered trademark and is used by Macmillan Publishing Group, LLC, under license from Pan Books Limited.

For book club information, please visit facebook.com/picadorbookclub or email marketing@picadorusa.com.

Library of Congress Cataloging-in-Publication Data

Names: Trubek, Anne, 1966– editor.
Title: Voices from the Rust Belt / edited and with an introduction
   by Anne Trubek.
Description: First edition. | New York : Picador, 2018. | Includes
   bibliographical references.
Identifiers: LCCN 2017040889 | ISBN 9781250162977 (trade paperback) |
   ISBN 9781250162984 (ebook)
Subjects: LCSH: Middle West—Economic conditions. | Middle West—
   Social conditions.
Classification: LCC HC107.A14 .V65 2018 | DDC 977'.034—dc23
LC record available at https://lccn.loc.gov/2017040889

Our books may be purchased in bulk for promotional, educational, or business use. Please contact your local bookseller or the Macmillan Corporate and Premium Sales Department at 1-800-221-7945, extension 5442, or by email at MacmillanSpecialMarkets@macmillan.com.

First Edition: April 2018

10 9 8 7 6 5 4 3 2 1

CONTENTS

GEOGRAPHY OF THE HEARTLAND

LEAVING AND STAYING

VOICES *from the* RUST BELT

INTRODUCTION

Why the Rust Belt Matters (and What It Is)

THE RUST BELT, LINGUISTICALLY SPEAKING, is one of America's newest regions. The name was largely created in 1984 by, of all people, Walter Mondale. At a campaign stop during the presidential election, Mondale made a speech to steelworkers at the LTV plant in Cleveland in which he decried Reagan's position on trade, particularly the lifting of quotas on steel imports, which had sent the industry into crisis. As he put it, "Reagan's policies are turning our industrial Midwest into a rust bowl."

The press tweaked Mondale's dust bowl reference into "Rust Belt," to make it play off "Sun Belt," another new term for an American region, this one coined in 1969 by Kevin Phillips in his book *The Emerging Republican Majority,* to describe a happier set of shifting demographics and economic policies. For over three decades since, the term has been deplored, praised, and parsed. There is a sizable contingent—especially among the baby boomers who remember the moment the term was coined—who consider it derogatory and strive to have it replaced (recent attempts to rebrand the region include the "Trust Belt, " the "New American Heartland," and the "Freshwater Region"). But the term has stuck.

Definitions of where, exactly, the Rust Belt is are also often debated[1]. There is no answer. The term was not invented by geographers but by a politician and the media. There are no natural borders, as there are with the East and West Coasts, say, or topographic features, as with the Great Plains or the Rocky Mountains. "Rust Belt" is a historical term, like "New England" and "Sun Belt" (even "Midwest" is as much historic as geographic). "Post-industrial Midwest" can serve as a synonym (along with its cousins, "industrial Midwest" and "formerly industrial Midwest"). Michigan, Ohio, and Pennsylvania are central to the region, as well as parts of Illinois, Wisconsin, and New York. "As far west as Milwaukee and as far east as Buffalo" usually works. Borderlands, such as Cincinnati and St. Louis, as well as abutting regions such as Appalachia, can be fun to debate over beers—just *how* rusty are they?—but in the end, anywhere an economy was previously based on manufacturing and has since been losing population can be part of the gang.

This is true internationally, too—China and Russia and Germany and just about any country with a history of manufacturing have rust belts where economies were once based on industry and now no longer are; least, that is how such declining regions are described in news headlines. Starting with the 2016 presidential election, the term was used more than it had been in recent memory by the American press, usually to describe the then-surprising popularity of Donald Trump and Bernie Sanders, who were campaigning, just like Walter Mondale before them, for more restrictive trade policies. Although Trump's support was strong in the South,

---

[1] http://beltmag.com/mapping-rust-belt

the West, and many areas of blue states like New York and California, Trump used the Rust Belt as an example of America's fall from prior greatness. Since the election, the term has continued to appear even more often in the mainstream media, usually in articles seeking to understand the appeal of Trump in the so-called Rust Belt region—again, despite Trump's equal or greater support elsewhere in the country.

The most common culprit for Rust Belt woes cited by politicians and the media is the North Atlantic Free Trade Agreement. And though NAFTA has become a popular political talking point, its impact on the region has been secondary. Mondale placed the blame on the policies of Ronald Reagan. But even earlier, in the 1970s, the demand for steel, which was high during World War II, had begun to wane, and many saw their jobs disappear. Arguably the most symbolic date in Rust Belt history was Black Monday, September 19, 1977, when Youngstown Sheet and Tube in Ohio closed down, leading to a loss of some forty thousand jobs[2]. Also notable: the region's population peaked in the 1970s and has been in decline ever since.

Those manufacturing jobs are never going to return to the levels seen in the 1970s. The lack of jobs and opportunity for the white working class has been an ongoing problem for over forty years now—long before Obama, Clinton, or even Reagan.

---

[2] http://www.museumofthecity.org/project/the-deindustrialization-of-youngstown/

And so the term "Rust Belt" continues to define the region, to the consternation of both those who have never liked it and those who wish the economy—any economy—would show up and turn "Rust Belt" from open sore to quaint artifact. And while the term may lack geographical strata, it has historical layers, and they are thick and redolent. The phrase is born of loss, but has acquired texture, depth, and decades' worth of meaning.

That more people have become curious about the Rust Belt since the 2016 presidential election is a welcome development. But it has become increasingly tempting—and increasingly dangerous—to reduce the Rust Belt to clichés. At a time when it is more important than ever to understand the nuances of this complex region, what is published instead are often articles on the "typical" Rust Belt resident—more often than not a white male Trump supporter. Generalizations about the region's population are now as popular as simply ignoring the Rust Belt was just a few years ago. Most are wrong.

Some important facts: Many Rust Belt cities have minority populations that statistically outpace those in other parts of the country. The largest per capita Muslim population in the United States is here, in Dearborn, Michigan. With so much emphasis placed on the manufacturing sector, many overlook the largest employers in the region: hospitals, retailers, and institutions of higher education. Of the handful of cities in the United States that support an Orthodox Jewish population, many are in the Rust Belt. A century ago, the region's cities were often populated primarily by non-native

English speakers. For example, in 1900, over 75 percent of the residents of Cleveland, Ohio, were foreign-born or first-generation immigrants.

To sum up such a diverse region with a few adjectives, or a rags-to-riches story of exceptionalism with a message of individualism at its core, is both misleading and dangerous. This book offers another way of looking at the Rust Belt, another way to grasp its contours—through dozens of individual stories, finely told. These essays address segregated schools, rural childhoods, suburban ennui, lead poisoning, opiate addiction, and job loss. They reflect upon happy childhoods, successful community ventures, warm refuges for outsiders, and hidden oases of natural beauty. But mainly they are stories drawn from uniquely personal experiences: A girl has her bike stolen. A social worker in Pittsburgh makes calls on clients. A journalist from Buffalo moves away and misses home. A city manager stops fighting the urge to relocate and decides to make a life in Akron. An ecologist takes her students to a CVS parking lot. A father gives his daughter a bath in the lead-contaminated water of Flint, Michigan.

We've come to recognize the major trends, popular as topics in opinion pages and stump speeches, that have come to shape the narrative of the region: racial discrimination, poverty, job loss, climate change, neglect, depopulation. But there is power in simply bearing witness. To learn about individual lives and specific places. To appreciate the writers' abilities to render experience. And to resist the urge to make of this place a static, incomplete cliché, a talking point, or a polling data set.

In lieu of a thesis or some prescription, these essays offer gorgeous turns of phrase, heartbreaking experiences, and raw emotion. There is an urgency to them. We have created not only income inequality but also narrative inequality in this nation: some stories are told over and over while others are passed over, muted. So the writers in this book seek you and say: *This is me and I am here.* But more, they say: *Please pay attention. Please listen. Let us tell you our story. We can tell it ourselves.*

The importance of paying attention is the tie that binds all the essays in this volume. It is also central to the mission of Belt Publishing—the press that initially published these pieces in *Belt Magazine* and in books on Detroit, Pittsburgh, Cleveland, Flint, Akron, and Buffalo—to create a much-needed space for the deep, various, complex, sad, wonderful, and pressing stories of the Rust Belt. The essays included here showcase the thick, overlapping, and various layers of the region. Like the Rust Belt, they are as suffused by life as they are by loss, if not more so.

—*Anne Trubek, founder and director of Belt Publishing*

GROWING UP

JACQUELINE MARINO

A Girl's Youngstown

I USED TO BE AFRAID of the mills, or what was left of them in the late 1970s. Although I grew up in Boardman, my family often went to visit my grandparents on the east side of Youngstown. As soon as we got to the Market Street Bridge, my sister and I would hit the floor of our mother's white Oldsmobile, clasping our hands over our noses and mouths. We would hold our breath until our lungs burned, until the structures we passed turned from smokestacks to skyscrapers.

My mother, a nurse, said the pollution the mills belched into the air made people sick and turned their lungs black. We didn't doubt her. All the old people we knew died of cancer. We weren't going to let that happen to us, though. When we saw the mills, we just wouldn't breathe.

Youngstown residents had been passing over the Market Street Bridge—most of them much more happily—since 1899. After being fought by farmers who didn't want to develop the city and "big interests" who thought the bridge would hurt them, its opening was "the climax of one of the most romantic chapters in the history of Youngstown," according to a 1914 article in The Sunday *Vindicator*. The number of homes on the south side increased from a few hundred in 1899 to several thousand fifteen years later. The number of schools more than doubled in that same time period, and the number of churches increased from two to ten. Toward the twentieth century's end, however, many journeys from the south side to downtown began reluctantly in the suburbs, whose residents, like us, were drawn not for business or fun but family obligation.

My sister and I continued holding our breath over that bridge throughout the 1980s, long after the mills closed. To us, the air was toxic and always would be. Those ugly structures were like sirens warning us to get to the air raid shelter. Mom would drive fast. We'd be blue, but safe.

As we got older, not breathing as we crossed into downtown became a form of protest. Going to Grandma's redbrick house on South Pearl Street seemed like a form of punishment. In the house, we did little besides play poker for pennies and watch network television. Outside, my grandpa's garden took up most of the backyard, and we weren't allowed to climb the cherry tree.

Our grandparents' neighborhood was nothing like ours in Boardman. We rode our bikes everywhere, sometimes even crossing Route 224 on our own. We explored the woods with our neighborhood friends, playing hide-and-seek and climbing trees until someone was thirsty or bleeding. Our lives were full and free. Cancer, black lungs, stinky mills—none of that Youngstown would touch us. We wouldn't let it.

I didn't realize then that you don't get to choose what parts of your hometown you get to claim any more than you can choose your grandmother's green eyes or your grand-

father's musical talent. You can't take the homemade ca-
vatelli and leave the corrupt politicians, or notice the Butler
art institute but not the ruins. The Youngstown of my past
is two cities: one safe, leafy, and full of promise; the other
scary, dirty, and stifling. In my memories, in me, both remain.

I have lived in a half dozen cities over the past twenty
years. I have appreciated and criticized them all for different reasons, but only Youngstown feels complicated. Perhaps it is complicated in the way all hometowns are. They
are the places where we learn to feel love and hate and the
spectrum of other meaningful emotions. But I think it's
different for those of us from Youngstown. Everything
about our city is heavy—steel, corruption, racial and class
division, and, most distinctively, the weight of others' con-
demnation.

Everyone carries it, even those of us without direct ties
to steel or organized crime. Neither Steeltown nor Crimetown had much claim on me. My parents were professionals, and my closest relatives to toil near the blast furnace
were great-uncles. As a girl, I didn't see myself in the history of a Youngstown everyone else seemed to know. Where
was my Youngstown? It would be many years before I would
realize no one had written its history yet.

At my grandparents' house, there was no thrill of dis-
covery in exploring the trappings of my mother's past. Almost nothing from my mother's girlhood remained—perhaps
because she had so little as a girl. Her tiny bedroom, at the
top of a flight of steep, narrow stairs, held only a single bed
and a dresser. I knew kids whose bedroom closets were
bigger. There was so little room, in fact, that the door only

opened about halfway before hitting the dresser. I didn't
know how my mother survived in that room. My bedroom
was my refuge, the place where I read and dreamed and wrote
in a household where no one except my father ever wanted
to be alone.

To write, fiction, Virginia Woolf said a woman needed
money and a room of her own. I think that's good advice
for anyone wishing to write anything, though I would add
another requirement: the room should be big enough for
a desk.

Growing up, my mother did not have money or a desk,
and she was rarely alone. Her one-bathroom, thousand-square-
foot house was shared with two younger brothers. My
grandparents were very social and their neighbors were
close. My mother remembers their community fondly. She
walked everywhere, waving at the neighbors sitting on their
front porches, engaged in the traditional Youngstown pastime
of street watching. She even walked to her school, Sacred
Heart, with its giant crucifix that towered over the mills.
In the early 1980s, however, we weren't allowed to leave
Grandma's brick driveway. When we went to Sacred Heart
for spaghetti dinners, we drove. The school was closed by
then and the church's crucifix had lost some of its majesty,
overlooking the ruins of the mills we used to hide from in
the Oldsmobile.

One by one, my grandparents' neighbors moved away
from Pearl Street. There were break-ins and drugs. Empty
liquor bottles and garbage littered the street. We rarely saw
other children there, only our cousins when they were visiting from other cities.

My grandparents left for Boardman in the 1980s, and I

didn't return to Pearl Street until nearly two decades later. I went back because Youngstown was haunting me. Once again, the city was at the center of something very bad on a national stage. By 2000, after a four-year investigation, the FBI had convicted dozens of people, including judges and other public officials, on corruption charges. Even Youngstown's congressman, James Traficant, was being investigated. It was like the worker uprisings of the 1910s, the mob wars of the 1960s, or the economic devastation of the 1970s. It didn't matter if you had nothing to do with any of that personally. If you were from Youngstown, you felt the heat.

Corruption in Youngstown wasn't just a onetime thing. It was "institutional," woven into the fabric of the city's culture. Or that's what everyone was saying, anyway. As a graduate student, I wanted to learn why. I went back to Youngstown to research the places where the city's history and my family's history intersected. I spent many hours over several months interviewing my relatives, including my grandparents. Even though I found no close relatives among the scores of Youngstown politicians, organized criminals, and lackeys who had been convicted over the years, I was amazed by the few degrees of separation between my family members and those who had given the city its disrepute.

These connections were often passing but memorable. My great-grandmother was shaken down for a gold pocket watch—the only thing of value belonging to her late husband—by a member of the Black Hand. Mobster Joseph "Fats" Aiellio, whose wife was one of my paternal grandmother's dearest friends, once gave my father a toy gun. (My grandmother, mortified, made him give it back.) My great-uncle Joe worked at the Calla Mar, a restaurant owned by Pittsburgh "godfather" Jimmy Prato, who threw a luncheon in honor of that grandmother when she died. At one time, almost everyone played the bug, the illegal gambling racket that perpetuated organized crime in Youngstown.

"Every day a guy would come to the house," my maternal grandmother, Betty D'Onofrio, told me. "You'd play three cents or five cents on a number."

Even I have a connection to a Youngstown criminal. Briefly in 1992, I interned for Congressman Traficant on Capitol Hill. After a full day of opening mail, answering phones, and greeting visitors, I asked one of his female aides when it would be my turn to shadow the chief of staff and attend receptions, like the only other intern—a man—had been doing all day. Her answer? Never.

"The congressman always wants a woman at the front desk," she said, with a contempt I hadn't expected. If I wanted to do anything else over the next three months, she strongly advised me to find another unpaid internship.

That was my last day.

The next week, I walked into the office of the National Women's Political Caucus, a nonpartisan group that works to get women elected to public office, and asked the communications director to hire me.

She did, but only after a closed-door meeting where she told me to strike the Traficant internship from my résumé.

"He's a laughingstock," she said. "This will follow you."

Nearly a decade later, while doing graduate research, I found myself interviewing mostly women, simply because they tend to outlive the men in my family. I tried to get them to tell me more about the people they knew who factored into Youngstown's criminal past, but instead they wanted to tell me about what their lives were like in the forties, fifties, and sixties. They told me about baking pizzas in outside brick ovens and the dangers of hanging your clothes out to dry on the clothesline in Brier Hill. (If the ash got on them, you'd have to wash them all over again.) My grandmother's family was so poor they lived off fried potatoes and whatever they could grow in the garden. Still, they prided themselves on raising good kids. Once, when my great-uncle stole a chicken, my great-grandmother said nothing.

"She just looked at him in a way that made him feel so guilty that he took it back," Grandma told me.

These family stories were entertaining, but what about the mob? The corrupt politicians? The thugs that wired car bombs and shot people? I inched the recorder closer.

"They never bothered us," she told me. "They knew we didn't have nothing."

I understand why Youngstown's wives, sisters, and daughters would want to forget the city's criminal past. It isn't really theirs; few women have emerged as perpetrators of the Crimetown USA image. In newspaper articles, they have been inconsequential characters, lightly sketched into the background, cooking or grieving. That's not to say they didn't know what was going on in back rooms and board-rooms, but you don't take too much ownership of the power structure when you're just greeting people at the front desk.

Here were those two Youngstowns again. Instead of the free and the scary, however, I saw distinct male and female views emerge in our much-maligned city. The male view resided in the realms of collapsed industry and crime. It is the one known and vilified by the rest of the world. The female view centered on family. Though loosely referred to in references to the city's ethnic roots, its strong loyalties and family values, that is not the story of Youngstown everyone else knows.

Despite the shame and defeatism many of us from Youngstown have felt, there is no badness in the blood here, no moral inferiority. There has been a historic lack of opportunity for half of us to speak for ourselves. Money and a room of their own? Few women in Youngstown had either.

To write a creative work, according to Woolf, writers should strive for "incandescence," the state of mind in which "there is no obstacle in it, no foreign matter unconsumed." You can only get to it if you're free, even temporarily, of the emotions spawned by dependent relationships, "grudges and spites and antipathies." Yet while we don't have to let our families in our rooms where we write, we must let them into our writing. Otherwise, no one will know our past. Steel and crime do not reflect our experience. The things we want to talk about in our eighties, those are real.

As much as I disliked going to my grandparents' house on Pearl Street, it always smelled good. I often ended up in the kitchen, where there were hard Italian cookies that never seemed to get stale and pots of sauce or wedding soup on the stove with my grandparents bustling around them, dropping handfuls of this or that into the pots, stopping only to let us kiss their pudgy cheeks and urge us to have something to eat. My grandparents' kitchen was as loving, happy, and gender-equal as any place I have ever been, definitely worth crossing the bridge for. I am sure it was just one of many oases in a turbulent city, but not recorded or celebrated as the special thing it was.

It's a small memory, but it feels good to write about it. Finally, I can breathe.

The Kidnapped Children of Detroit

IT HAPPENED SUDDENLY.

One day, we'd be outside with our friends, black, brown, and white, on the warm summer days before the start of the next school semester, playing jacks and hopscotch, riding bikes.

The next day, our white friends would be gone. One of my friends might have said, "Hey, we're moving," in the middle of a game of kickball, but there were few real good-byes, or promises to keep in touch, at least not of the type associated with the farewells of kids who had been together all or most of their lives.

In the jumbled mishmash of childhood memories during those transitional years, I recall worshipers leaving the neighborhood church after Sunday service, descending the dark oak staircase from the sanctuary. In their hurry to get on with their day, it looked, from my kid-level gaze, like a stampede, during those late-summer days when our integrated neighborhood was disassembling before my eyes. I will forever associate the Sunday-dressed hemlines and dark-suited pant legs with their rushing, running to get away—from us—the worshipers with whom they had just fellowshipped before God.

White parents were grabbing their kids and escaping from Detroit—and from its enclave Highland Park, where I grew up, a then solidly middle-class community within Detroit's borders, "a city within a city." Often, it appeared as if they left in the dark of the night; the moves seemed so clandestine. This sense of them leaving virtually "overnight," packing up and disappearing, was likely due to the white parents' reluctance to speak to their black neighbors—whom they often treated with pronounced neighborliness—about their impending moves, given that their departures were largely because of the color of the neighbors' skin.

I wonder if some worried that their daytime public neighborliness contrasted with their nighttime kitchen table planning, their plotting to get out of the neighborhood as soon as they could manage. Perhaps they forbade their children to speak to their darker friends about the frenetic packing going on inside. Certainly they didn't want to speak of the reason for the moves—though everyone, of course, knew why. Or they talked to their black neighbors pretending "those new people moving in" didn't include those with whom they commiserated. But one by one, the white families left their old homes, tree-lined streets—and us—behind.

I'm sure that some of my friends listened to their parents in their homes, as they spoke of us with words of racial hatred, while outside they smiled across backyard fences, making small talk about sod and azaleas. Perhaps black and white neighbors rarely communicated at all during this time, when our neighborhoods were soon to be re-segregated. For there was virulent racism and ill-disguised violence in areas throughout the city, and even in the late sixties, blacks could not shop in many stores. Detroit's history was replete with episodes of unrest and even terror in the competition over housing: whites demanded that blacks be stopped from moving into an east side housing project, which precipitated a race riot in 1943. A generation before that, Ossian Sweet, a black medical doctor, was met with mobs as he moved into his home in a white neighborhood on the near east side. Clarence Darrow would defend Sweet's right to defend his hearth, and establish, "A man's home is his castle."

My grandmother told me the tale of how, in the early fifties, she had saved up the money she made as a domestic to buy a home on Clairmont and Woodward avenues. On the eve of the closing, the realtor came to her with the news that the white block club did not want her in the neighborhood. Grandmother refused to change her plans and sent him packing, but the realtor returned—the block club offered to pay her back the money for her down payment, plus some. Grandmother took the money and ran, to a neighborhood on the near east side.

She moved near Conant Gardens, a community developed on land that had been owned by an abolitionist named Shubael Conant, who refused to sell his land to developers who sold homes with the restrictive covenants that were common in Detroit. That community was one of the first strongholds of black middle-class home ownership. My grandmother chuckled at the end of her story, at the irony that by the time of her telling, thirty years later, Clairmont and Woodward was all black—the block club had obviously been unable to buy its way against the changing times.

Some whites, I'm sure, were not influenced by race baiting, but left the city solely to experience the new suburban living, or to be closer to the jobs that had moved across 8 Mile—though they knew that they were going to communities where blacks were not allowed. Some of my friends' parents were surely anguished about the decision to move, sometimes leaving behind equity and often their own parents, who refused to go. Did my young white friends listen to their planning with conflicted feelings? Never mind; the torrent of change and fear that was driving white Detroiters could not be turned off.

And so, I say my friends were kidnapped; snatched away from their homes, often under cover of night or in rushed moves that split us apart for a lifetime. I watched Mary Martin fly as Peter Pan on TV, and it seemed my friends, too, had been lured to a Neverland. Did they cry when they were taken, missing their old friends? Did they think of what they'd left behind when they woke in homes with no deep porches or rich oaken banisters? On streets with no lush, ancient trees? Where it took a car—or two—to get anywhere, with lawns so new that grass had yet to grow? But my friends settled into their new neighborhoods, like children do, adapting and making friends, happy for the new. Glad to be in the modern houses on spread-out blocks, out of the brick behemoths, two-family flats, or frame houses of the old, dense Detroit streets they'd left behind.

One of my friends remembers the overwhelming fear that consumed his family's 7 Mile and Wyoming household—a relatively new community even then—as they prepared to leave for Southfield. He confirms that, as in so many homes, there was a sense of panic as his family prepared not just to move but to escape, as if from some impending debacle. He recalls how, in the innocence of youth, he wondered about the reason for the terror; for it appeared to him that the black folks moving into his neighborhood were at the very least, in his child's-eye view of social class, the most non-scary folks in the world: doctors, teachers, professionals. To him, they seemed to be of a clearly higher social standing than most of the folks who were desperately moving out.

It happened rapidly. An elder of my church remembers that he started school in his west-side neighborhood as only one of two black children in his kindergarten class; the rest were white, mostly Jewish. By the time he left elementary school, only two white children remained. The Jewish exodus (so to speak) was an integral engine of the movement of blacks across the west side, for they were willing to break the "restrictive covenants" in deeds that had prohibited home-owners from selling to blacks, and often Jews, too. Block by block, as whites moved out, Jewish homeowners replaced them and then blacks followed, with synagogues transformed into black churches.

After the 1967 riots (also known as the Rebellion, in which my own father's record business was destroyed), the post-conflagration trauma was so great, and the consciousness of Detroiters so altered by the eruption of turmoil and destruction, that it came to be said that "all the white people left after sixty-seven," a false narrative that persists even today. In reality, the exit from the city began after World War II. By 1952, construction of Northland Center mall in suburban Southfield had begun, to accommodate the mounting loss of population from Detroit; it became the first and largest suburban mall in the country. Whites bought new houses in the newly built suburbs, when the schools in the city were still quite good; and really, there was no reason to go except for a change of scenery and a good use of the G.I. Bill. But blacks were straining against the "James Crow" segregation of the North, and out of the packed neighborhoods in which they had been confined. Millions of whites were worked into moving-van frenzy by word of mouth from one home to the other, and in rabble-rousing community meetings. Importantly, real estate interests and developers—often individually, and surely cumulatively—stood to profit greatly from that rapid turnover of properties.

Some real estate companies grew rich from this race-based trading in hope and fear. Some actually identified neighborhoods and instigated the whole cycle in order to profit from the terror-driven turnover of properties. One of my friends remembers when her white neighborhood was inundated with flyers exhorting whites to get away from the coming dark hordes. Neighborhoods had brief, uneasy periods of "integration," marked by racial tension and police brutality, before the last of the whites would move out.

This practice is called "block-busting," creating a crazy, predictable cycle—whites move out, lured by real estate interests to leave for white communities; blacks move in and fear is escalated; whites become panicked and, egged on by the realtors and block associations, sell at ever lower prices in order to hurry and "get out." This also happened when blacks moved into communities paying higher rents or land-contract prices than the whites before them. The more whites that moved out, "dumping" houses onto the market, the more blacks were able to move in; many of them were on a lower

economic rung than those who preceded them, creating a
self-fulfilling prophecy.

The result—a neighborhood that had solidly middle
class or even affluent blacks and whites now had, in a few
short years, a preponderance of poorer families. These were
families who were often less able to maintain the lifestyle
previously enjoyed in that neighborhood, and brought with
them the problems their children often had in rough projects or poorer communities. Many of my black friends from
harsher backgrounds had a difficult time adjusting to the
quiet, tree-lined life on their new blocks. In each neighborhood, they used the drugs that were flooding into the communities to deal with their anxieties of being planted in
these short-lived "mixed" communities, where they were often
not wanted by blacks or whites. This accelerated the neighborhood's crime and disruption—the final death knell for
many communities.

Another factor I remember that prompted moves to the
suburbs was violence, whether threatened or carried out,
against white kids, who were often tormented by black kids
in outbursts of retaliation for wrongs real or imagined. Later,
there was the busing of children to schools as a tactic to
address the re-segregation of the community, with the rise
of agitators who whipped up a frenzy of racial fear and
hatred, driving whites further across 8 Mile. A group of us
stared down Klan sympathizers on the east side, singing
"We Shall Overcome" in the streets during chilling episodes
of anti-busing turmoil.

As people left, so did businesses; the suburbs, an appealing, all-white commercial for modern living, were a vacuum
sucking life and enterprise across 8 Mile. Many of the larg-

est industrial enterprises had gone first, finding in the un-developed suburbs the acres of land needed for the modern, stretched-out production facilities that could not be built in the property-dense city. Companies left behind the tight neighborhoods where residents could and did join organizing efforts of all kinds, and by the 1960s, there was a freeway system to move out workers and supplies. Detroit's infra-structure, dependent upon the former booming tax base and not the new, shrinking one, was less able to maintain services. With joblessness that became epidemic, and the ruination of great sections of the social fabric via the scourge of crime and drugs, the urban community spiraled ever downward.

This circular, self-fulfilling, nasty game of musical chairs perpetuated itself in the Detroit area, as in other "changing" communities nationwide. As whites departed en masse, the problems they most feared came to pass. In many areas, blacks moved into communities that they were suddenly allowed to afford, yet they were unable, in the long run, to maintain this new life. Or, blacks with means moved into communities with aged housing stock, making the next years of living a fait accompli of devastation. Later, the mortgage crisis sealed the deal of destruction in many neighborhoods.

Even so, after white flight, there were still many commu-nities full of dedicated residents who were paragons of home-ownership, with houses and lawns maintained in consummate displays of steadfast residential pride, despite the challenges of living in the midst of flight and escalating blight. Detroit still has exquisite blocks in affluent neighborhoods, and handsome, solid homes on working-class blocks—maintained by those who remained. My own neighborhood, Lafayette

Park, was built in 1960 to staunch the flow of white Detroiters outward. It is still a model of diverse urban living, with those who live there committed to the city.

During the departures in the late sixties, my next-door neighbors were among the last whites to leave our block; we had lived next door to them all of our lives. He was president of a bank on Woodward Avenue, and on the verge of retirement, but I guess the changing times had become too much; whites were now moving at the sound of the drumbeat of the Black Power era. The banker's wife, a white-haired lady who had known me since I was a babe, literally burst into tears across the backyard fence at the sight of my brand-new sixties Afro, and asked me tearfully why I had to wear my hair "like that." Shortly after, it was time for them to go. Some whites waited too long and moved into communities in which they were branded by the stigma of having come from neighborhoods that had long ago turned black, and were therefore never to be viewed as really equal to the other whites in their new towns.

But they were all transfigured into new souls called suburbanites, though many maintained an undying love-hate relationship with the neighborhoods they were forced by fear to leave behind, often viewing the city and its current residents with a mixture of contempt, dismay, and nostalgia. They pined for the old glory days of the city, following the stories of its streets and politics as if they lived within its boundaries; following the news of its decline like a lover both grieving and gloating over the travails of a lost love. In the late sixties, many of my black friends began to leave, too, as the city declined, for segregation had finally lifted its weight from the close-lying suburbs. So they, too, moved across 8 Mile.

Over the years, I've known many whites who work in downtown Detroit and savor the scary, sexy power of being comfortable in the city—at least during work hours. They're proud of their ability to move around the urban landscape and to have at least daytime friends of other colors. Most whites in the Detroit area stay away, however, especially from anywhere outside of downtown, fearful of the community beyond it. But some former Detroiters are pulled back to their old neighborhoods—some intact, some bedraggled, some where the old home is completely gone: the decay and destruction an affirmation of their parents' obviously right decision to leave, so long ago.

I wonder if, sometimes, they suspect that decision itself, multiplied across Detroit, was at least part of the cause of all the mess here now. That maybe the mass flight, the leaving of property all over town, the years of being egged on by whispers and realtors to cross 8 Mile, was all part of a nasty, self-destructive Monopoly game involving real properties and real lives. I wonder what might have happened in Detroit if there had never been this flight—if whites had held on and resisted the racial manipulation; if blacks had been able to push back the plague of unemployment, drugs, and crime; if we had been able to live in Detroit, all at one time.

It is hard for many black Detroiters to comprehend the sense of belonging, or even entitlement, that many whites feel toward Detroit, even decades and states removed from living within the city boundaries. There are those—black and white—who have never lived in Detroit proper, or even in Michigan, who gaze (through Google Maps) at old family homesteads, and vicariously traverse old family blocks from afar. They regard Detroit as their city. And I believe that the sense of being part of Detroit proper—despite living well outside of its borders for generations—is rooted in that mass evacuation. Like the movement of blacks across the city after the destruction of Black Bottom—a predominantly black neighborhood razed in the early sixties in the name of urban renewal—this was an unprecedented transfer of community; and suburban parents did their best, as they understood it, to build better lives. But fear of a black city made my friends Detroiters in exile.

Folks ask the question, *Will Detroit come back?* Well, Detroit never left—but three generations did. Today, regardless of the city's efforts at redevelopment, most know that they will never again live in the city of their affection. Most of the old neighborhoods are much too far from livability for them, and the city's core and urban lifestyle holds no appeal for those accustomed to suburban sprawl. But more and more of the children and grandchildren of the Kidnapped Children are finding their way home. Yet despite ghost-town metaphors, "blank slate" pronouncements, and prairie-land descriptions of Detroit, they find the city already occupied, and these strangers in a strange yet familiar land must learn to share it with those who held on.

As the quality of life in the outer ring of the city declined, forcing more blacks to look outward to escape crime and to seek neighborhood stability, property values fell in the near suburbs—because of the age of those communities and their housing stock, because of the mortgage crisis, because of block-busting that is still alive and well (though sometimes with more subtle practices than before). As many of the suburbs become less "exclusive" and downtown living grows, owners who held on to core city properties during the crash of their values watch their fortunes rise, after contributing to the city's vistas of decay and destruction. For decades, they held on to ravaged, abandoned structures as they waited for a time of profitability, contributing to much of the urban devastation for which black city dwellers have been reviled.

Younger generations of whites from the suburbs, who don't have their forebears' fear of the city, are moving in the opposite direction, proudly proclaiming their Detroit provenance and reveling in their new urban life. Some of them re-create suburban segregation in the heart of the city; they want life in Detroit—without Detroiters. But many more look to the city as the most exciting place in the world to live in diversity. They are led by the artists' community, the creative seraphim of redevelopment; they are the coal-mine canaries of our scorched and burned land. This community of artists has been waiting and creating for such a time as this, for Detroit has always been a city of artists. Our extreme creative impulse in Detroit is now unfettered, no longer consumed by the past that propelled, yet devoured, so much of the city's creative energy. The artists are side by side with those who've held on for decades, trying to make "a way out of no way."

As in South Africa, there is a need for atonement in Detroit and its suburbs. We need a restorative movement to heal what has happened here, as the working people of this town competed against themselves over the right to the good life. We have to share stories about the experiences of the past era. As we move forward in Detroit, there must be a mending of the human fabric that was rent into municipal pieces with the divisions of city and suburbs. Small, continual acts of reconciliation are called for here, as sections of the city rise again.

As the children and grandchildren of the Kidnapped Children make their way to the city, I believe that it is the responsibility of the rest of us—those who, like me, never left—to welcome them; to tell our new residents the real city narratives, to share the truths of what happened here from all sides. There are deep schisms that never should have been, that were orchestrated by self-serving interests; we must work to mend these wherever possible. Our new residents have a contagious earnestness, energy, and hopefulness, reminiscent of the movements of our past, and there's a difference between their sincere efforts for change and the machinations of those who would manipulate the urban crisis to their own benefit, casting us aside like flotsam in the name of progress.

Yet it is likewise the charge of our new Detroiters to acknowledge and respect those already here—to actually see longtime residents, for we are not invisible. Our new residents must learn from our history and experience; they must work alongside our earlier residents and their children in Detroit's renewal, for they are the bedrock of the redeveloped city and the nexus of its future. Let us figure out—this time—how to live together, so that more children and grandchildren of the Kidnapped Children can come home to live in the city, so that more of our children and grandchildren might also be part of a truly new Detroit. Young

people come to be freed from their lives of suburban isola-
tion and the crippling divisions of this region; they want to
be a part of a new urban reality. It is true that some say that
they have come to save Detroit, but I say, they come to Detroit to *be* saved.

AMANDA SHAFFER

Busing, a White Girl's Tale

THE CUDELL/EDGEWATER NEIGHBORHOOD WHERE I grew up was a land of immigrant hyphens in the 1970s: Italian-American, Irish-American, Polish-American, and Hungarian-American, just to name a few. Folks who didn't fit any of these "ethnic categories" had come to Cleveland from Pennsylvania, West Virginia, and Kentucky to find work, and still called those other places "goin' back home." At the time, everyone I knew was Catholic; the Indian kids were actually Lakota, and no one had heard of diversity. Black History Month had just been invented and Martin Luther King Jr. Day didn't exist yet. It's easy to forget how different life was. Once upon a time, it was all I knew.

In 1976, the Honorable Frank J. Battisti ruled that Cleveland schools were racially segregated. When the Cleveland public school system implemented desegregation three years later, I was in middle school.

Desegregation meant that black kids would be bused across town to white schools, white kids would be bused to the black schools, and the Puerto Rican kids from the near West Side went in both directions. Busing meant that, for the first time, there was going to be more than one black kid in my school.

I don't remember the angry demonstrations and protests that reportedly took place, as my family weren't really march-in-the-streets people. As friends reported how their parents were putting them in parochial or private schools, my mother stuck to her "we are all God's children under the skin" party line. She was a woman of deep faith and little money. While all five of my siblings attended Catholic school, I had somehow persuaded my parents to allow me to attend public. When busing went into effect, my parents offered me Catholic high school and again I refused.

The first phase of busing reassigned some students for ninth grade, their last year of middle school. I wasn't one of them, which meant I'd be bused for all of high school. In September 1979, I entered ninth grade at Wilbur Wright Junior High School with only half the white kids who had attended with me the year before. Very little voluntary mixing with new students took place; in true teen fashion, everyone stuck with their crowd. There were quite a few after-school fights and a lot of assemblies about getting along with each other. I made one black friend that year. She seemed to slide into our group seamlessly.

In the summer of 1980, I found out I would be attending John Hay High School in a part of town I had only visited once before, on a school field trip to the Cleveland Museum of Art Armor Court. That summer, the majority of the kids I'd attended school with my entire life were being transferred to Griswold Academy, which everyone referred to as "Freedom Academy." Apparently they weren't opposed to attending an unaccredited school and taking a GED to graduate, as long as it was all-white.

I probably should have been more worried when school started, but I worked very hard to be blasé and super-cool about the whole thing. I felt sophisticated and tough. Ready for anything. I'm sure there was a fat manila envelope delivered in the weeks leading up to the first day of school full of instructions and supply lists and emergency medical forms, but all I remember is receiving the train tickets.

Attending John Hay meant taking the Rapid Transit train to school instead of a school bus. I had only taken the Rapid a handful of times to go downtown to Higbee's with my older sister to shop and get a Frosty. Now getting to school every day would mean a walk to the Rapid, a wait for the Rapid, a ride on the Rapid, and then a walk to the school from the University Circle station. This required careful coordination in the morning so no one in our friend group would have to ride alone. Because we were too cool to ride the shuttle from the Rapid to Hay, a daily highlight was crossing the four lanes of rush-hour traffic on Carnegie in the morning. While everyone else made a mad dash, my girlfriend and I would stroll, slowly and belligerently, giving drivers attitude as we crossed against the light.

At first glance, compared to West Tech High School, which held close to four thousand students, John Hay was small and shabby. And it came with a security guard at the door who checked our IDs every morning. The ID-checking lasted for a few weeks at the beginning of each year and then was abandoned with a laxness that would be unheard-of now in our post-Columbine world. Then again, it was probably easy to remember twenty white kids in a class of 144.

Inside the classroom, I was back in the majority, as the 13 percent of white students translated into 87 percent of the class through the magic of honors courses. The sorting started early in my school career. In second grade, I was classified into what was called "Major Works," and promptly started learning French. My friends and I, with the brutality of the young, broke it down to "smart kids" and "dumb kids." There must have been Major Works in the all-black schools, too, but all through high school my honors classes had a majority of white students.

The only class without an honors section was tenth-grade Black Literature, one of the most miserable experiences I can remember in twelve years of schooling. Not because of the content, which at that time was new to me, but because the teacher usually taught the "dumb kids" so the class read aloud from the book one paragraph at a time. Being a "smart kid" meant I'd never experienced such a thing, nor did I know that some kids read so poorly they counted ahead on the paragraphs so they could practice before their turn. Being as snotty and dismissive as I could get away with, I arrogantly propped novels inside my book during this class, reading anything to distance myself from the reality. This class may be what folks imagine Cleveland public schools are like, but, aside from it, my reality was AP English, honors French, and chemistry. I got a fine education, graduated from college, earned a master's degree, and am now a contributing member of society like most of the rest of the class of 1983, who became lawyers, teachers, business owners, and professional athletes.

The real education happened outside of class.

Growing up in a working-class, gendered household in

the 1970s turned me into a feminist before I knew what to call it. The concept of "women's work" and "men's work" was just the tip of the patriarchal iceberg. As a baby feminist, I was highly attuned to sexist behavior and prejudice against women. What I had never paid any attention to was what it was like to be a minority. I had never noticed that my father called black kids "pickaninnies" or that my brother called Puerto Ricans "spics." I didn't see other kinds of oppression and discrimination. I didn't know what I didn't know.

The first week of school I had trouble with a couple of black girls giving me a hard time, making comments under their breath and sucking their teeth at me. I don't remember what started it or brought it to a head, but back then I wasn't capable of backing down from a confrontation. Bumping turned into shoving, which turned into books slammed to the floor and then stepping up. Thankfully, the assistant principal magically appeared in that way that they do, shut it down, and pulled me into his office. He listened to my outrage at the unjust and unprovoked attack, and kindly explained to me what had happened. The hard stare and tough attitude that I thought said "Don't challenge me" was interpreted here as "I challenge you."

As ignorant as it sounds to be sixteen and not recognize that, this was the first time I glimpsed another culture. At sports events, I became one of two white girls on the black side of the bleachers and suddenly could see the unease, wariness, and race consciousness of the all-white teams.

The shifts in my perspective were slow but steady, and shaped who I am today. Walking around in my white skin, even female white skin, gave me the privilege not to see, not to hear, if I didn't want to. Now that I knew some black people, I could hear comments like "Wipe that pop can; you don't know if a black person touched it" for what they were—casual, deeply ingrained prejudice. I started to feel ashamed and embarrassed that my family and neighbors had these racist beliefs. And of myself, that I had never questioned them.

An undisputed benefit of court-ordered busing, among other things, was being given the opportunity to experience what it is like to be in the minority. Just a taste. I would never claim, because of this or any other experience, to know what it's like to be a minority in Cleveland or anywhere else. I will never live in brown skin and cannot know. What I was given, and what I am grateful for, was the chance to understand how narrow and limited my worldview was before I spent three years crossing the mighty Cuyahoga to attend school.

If I hadn't been bused, would it have bothered me when my brother sat with a shotgun on his front porch to "keep the black kids off the grass"? An equal-opportunity hater, he hated Jews, spics, niggers, towel heads, and gooks and never missed an opportunity to share his opinions. Busing meant groups of black kids got off the Rapid every day and had to walk past his house to get to West Tech. Seeing as he worked third shift at the factory, 8:00 A.M. would find him drinking beer on his front porch with his shotgun across his knees to stare down the black kids.

I never witnessed him with his gun, but I remember when he told me how he was "dealing with busing." He was so gleeful that the kids looked scared. I left his house that day feeling sick. I don't think I really believed that racism was "that big of a deal" before that day. It had seemed abstract, harmless, and deep in the past.

Not everyone had a good experience, even the other kids in our class. In fact, seventeen of the twenty white kids held their own after-prom over on the West Side. The rest of us danced at Vel's to "Atomic Dog."

Many people still blame busing for "ruining" the Cleveland schools, but for me the experience of getting out of my neighborhood was life-altering and incredibly positive. I consider myself lucky. Being bused is the reason I live in a racially and socioeconomically diverse neighborhood and send my child to public school. It's why I attempt to strive for equity and racial and social justice in any work I do. I am grateful, not to be white in America, but to know that I am.

JEFF Z. KLEIN

North Park, With and Without Hate

WALK DOWN HERTEL AVENUE AND see the mix of cultures: hipster cafés and old Italian red-sauce restaurants and halal butchers and louche interior design stores and pubs where young Americans have decided they're huge Barça fans. Maybe even a rainbow flag here and there. Walk down the side streets. The houses are filled with young families, different cultures—middle class, not rich, not poor—fresh ground coffee, organic groceries, craft beer.

Funny, though—it still looks exactly the way it did half a century ago. All the two-story houses. The attics topped by the same triangular or square roofs. The little backyards. The narrow driveways just wide enough to accommodate a Model T (from another fifty years before, when the houses were built). The five- or six-stair stoops. The trees shading the street, almost as tall and domelike as the elms whose arching boughs formed vast, block-long ceilings, like a great green cathedral. Late at night, the train horns, blaring distant and lonely from the raised embankments on either margin of the neighborhood.

The winter. Walking to school on the snowbanks. Bombing cars with snowballs. Grabbing the rear bumper of some unsuspecting Dodge and pogeying down the snow-covered street.

Jew.

Buffalo, the United States, the world, was different. Pinched. Small. Mean. North Park was made up entirely of white people—Catholics, Protestants, and a significant minority of Jews; no one else—and that made it just about the most diverse neighborhood in the city. There were two cuisines: regular food (meat and potatoes) and Italian food (spaghetti and pizza). We had a third, kosher. Separate sets of dishes and silverware, no mixing of milk and meat, no pork, no ham, no bacon.

That was one of the things that set them off.

You've never had ham? You think you're too good for it, don't you.

I had two best friends when I was a little boy, James M. and Freddie C. They were cool with me, but their brothers called me Hambone, in honor of the dietary habits of the Jews. Freddie was a couple years older than me. He and I would debate who was better, the Beatles or the Dave Clark Five. He loved the Beach Boys, and we both thought "Help Me, Rhonda" might be the best song ever. James was a good football player, touch or tackle. We followed the Bills closely. Jack Kemp or Daryle Lamonica? Against the Boston Patriots, should they give the ball to Cookie Gilchrist on every play?

The other sport that mattered was baseball. James and his family liked the San Francisco Giants. My family and I liked the L.A. Dodgers. My father was from Brooklyn. My sister was born there. And I liked Sandy Koufax because he was the best pitcher in baseball and wouldn't play that

World Series game on Yom Kippur. I had his baseball card. So James's older brother John is standing next to the stoop and asks if he can see my Sandy Koufax card. I hand it down to him. He takes it and rubs the face of it, hard, on the iron railing, up and down, several times. Here, he says, handing it back to me. Koufax's picture is still there, but it's got black streaks all over it.

The food especially seemed to get to them. The older C. and M. brothers simply could not get over their impression that keeping kosher meant Jews thought Catholic meat was inferior and couldn't be eaten. One day when my mother wasn't home, the M. brothers asked if they could come inside and get a snack out of the kitchen. I let them in and they descended on the fridge and cabinets like locusts, devouring all the Wise potato chips and Ritz crackers and Hershey bars they could find. But their real motivation was simply to see what the kitchen of Jews looked like.

"Not so different," one of them said. "Where's the kosher stuff?"

I don't want this to sound like a bitter catalog of slights from the musty scrapbook of my childhood. That's not my point. It's just that we've gotten into the habit of extolling the tight-knit ethnic enclaves of long ago, conveniently omitting one of their distinguishing characteristics—they could be snake pits of hatred. It didn't matter who the majority was, and it didn't matter who the Other was. The majority actively hated the Other. That's the way it was in most neighborhoods, in most cities. Yet, despite that, those neighborhoods could be wonderful. North Park—the old North Park, not the one now, which I like, but I'm talking about the old one—that North Park was a great place to be a kid.

But there was this one thing. It kept coming up.

Once I went over to Freddie's house down the block, the C. house. His two or three older brothers seemed surprised to see me.

Hambone, what are you doing here?

They stood around in the living room, ostentatiously discussing politics. Hitler, he was bad. But he had some good ideas. A look at me to gauge my reaction. These were fifteen-, seventeen-, and twenty-year-olds talking in front of a nine-year-old. I think one of their parents told them to stop, but I might be making that part up. I do recall unmistakably their banter, their laughter, and how it went on long enough to make me uncomfortable. I knew full well what Hitler had done. It had happened only twenty years earlier.

My mother could sense the anti-Semitism in the air of our neighborhood, and she hated it. She'd grown up in Toronto when Toronto was the polar opposite of what it is today. When she was a girl, there'd been a riot, Gentiles versus Jews, at the Christie Pits playing fields over the display of a swastika flag. At the beaches on the other side of town, some swim clubs flew swastikas to keep the Jews out. NO JEWS NEED APPLY signs at job sites were common. All that institutionalized anti-Semitism when she was growing up, and then the Nuremberg Laws and World War II and the camps. She had reason to suspect Jew-hatred everywhere she looked, but I scoffed—I thought what she experienced had gotten to her and made her obsessive. Many years later, we were watching TV together, and we saw a universally respected statesman disembark from a plane for a peacekeeping mission at some international trouble spot.

"Look at that anti-Semite," she said.

"What are you talking about?" I said dismissively. "That's the secretary general of the UN."

It was Kurt Waldheim. Later we learned he'd been an SS officer during the war. My mother was right; the old world was full of them.

She'd claim that things in our neighborhood got worse around Easter. I never noticed, but I do remember the only time in my childhood that I heard the phrase "You killed Christ." It came from one of James's older brothers on a spring day. I didn't understand. *What?*

You killed Christ. Well, not you, but your people.

I was completely baffled. I didn't know the story. I asked my mother.

"This is what they teach them in their churches," she said. She named the church down the block. "They teach this every Easter, and people like the C.'s and the M.'s come out and act worse than they usually do."

I asked my father, too, but he just shrugged it off. He'd grown up in a place where all the ethnicities blended without incident, and he simply didn't care. He was an architect and an FDR Democrat through and through, and he never had a bad word to say about any group. (The last job he did was to convert an old East Side church building into a mosque, and that was after 9/11. He was friendly with the imam. I thought the whole thing was pretty remarkable. I wanted to write an article about it for a Buffalo magazine, and after much hemming and hawing the magazine editor got back to me. "Well, it's like this," the guy said. "A lot of people we talked to don't think what your father did is necessarily a good thing." Jerk.)

If you weren't around in the 1960s, you may not truly

understand how pervasive this stuff was. People then didn't veil their prejudices—they were all out in the open, and nothing to be particularly embarrassed about. This was a time of ubiquitous Polack jokes, or, as sanitized on TV by famous comedians, "Polish jokes." No Asian immigration was allowed, so there simply were no Asians around, but there was plenty of talk about the Japs in World War II. And the N-word wasn't something you heard on TV, but it was pretty common in casual conversation. One of the older M. brothers spoke of a kid he knew who was a great football player. "He's a n—, but I tell you, I respect him," he said.

We grunted gravely in agreement, acknowledging how sincere and important an assertion this was. I tried saying the word a couple of times, but even back then it sounded foul; now I can't even type it, and you'd be mortified to see it in print. I can't remember the kid's name, but he came over once and played football with us. He was the only black kid who set foot in our neighborhood in the thirteen years I lived there.

One day when I was eleven or twelve, I went out our front door and heard a tremendous amount of yelling from the C. house. It seemed to be directed across the street, where a family of Hasidic Jews, although I didn't know the term at the time, were moving in. They looked exotic. We and all the other Jews we knew were totally secular and assimilated—no yarmulkes, no outward sign of Jewishness. But these guys in their black suits and black hats, they stood out. Still, I couldn't figure out what was going on.

I walked over to the C.'s porch. The older C. and M. brothers were there, huddling behind the railings, yelling,

"Get out! Get out!" They'd spring up and throw small stones at the Hasids hauling chairs and couches into their new house, then duck down again behind the cover of the railing. I can't remember if James or Freddie was there. Maybe I don't want to. But I do remember, quite vividly, asking, "What are you doing? Why are you doing this?" One of the older brothers answered.

Look at them. We don't want them living here.

He seemed to forget that I was one of them, too. He sprang up and threw another stone, and so did a couple of others. They yelled across the street, "Get out, you Jews!"

For many years I blamed myself for not saying anything at that moment, but now I understand that I responded within the boundaries of the behavior that had always worked for me: I simply left the porch and walked away. They kept screaming at the Hasids, who kept moving their furniture in without responding to the taunts or the stones, and they were still screaming as I stepped through my front door. But something in me had changed. I never talked to the C.'s or the M.'s again. Not even James or Freddie, even though I thought then, and still think now, that they never shared the hatred that their older brothers spewed.

The Hasidic family moved away just a month or two later, and after another year, so did we, to Eggertsville. Officially we could be counted as part of the white flight fleeing Buffalo, like all the whites leaving cities for the suburbs across late-sixties America. But in our case, that'd be misleading. We weren't fleeing black people, or poverty, or crime, or declining city services. We were fleeing the M.'s and the C.'s, to the northern suburbs, where the other Jews lived.

So the first week I'm at my new suburban junior high school, and a kid comes up to me and asks, "Are you Jewish?" Uh-oh, here we go, I think to myself.

"I am—does that affect anything?" I answer, challengingly. I think at this point I'm finally ready to fight.

But the kid is totally normal. "Oh no," he says. "I was just curious."

And that was it. From the moment we moved to Eggertsville, I never heard an anti-Jewish slur again. And in the five decades since, living in Manhattan and L.A., and now, just off Allen Street in Buffalo, nothing. I've heard Jews say bad things about other people, but never the other way around.

It seems like everything turned way back there, in the 1960s, thanks to Vatican II, which changed church theology to stop blaming the Jews for the crucifixion of Christ; and thanks, too, to the civil rights movement, the feminists, new immigration laws that permitted Asians and Africans to come to the United States, Stonewall and the gay rights movement, and, all in all, to the very slowly dawning recognition that everyone deserves dignity and respect.

I recognize that what I experienced in my childhood was not all that difficult, and certainly nothing compared to what most black people can tell you about their experiences—or First Nations people, or Latinos, or Asians, or those in the LGBTQ community. And as I write this, a guy running for president wants to ban Muslims from entering the country. I recognize that we're definitely a long way from utopia.

But now, when I walk down Hertel Avenue, I feel all right. My old neighborhood may look the same, but it has definitely changed. No slurs, no hate, no threats. The only sounds are the music streaming from the bars, the happy shouts of the soccer fans, and the rustling leaves in the boughs arched high overhead, the great green cathedral that shelters everyone.

DAVID FAULK

Moundsville

THERE IS A STORY THAT has circulated my hometown like an intractable conspiracy theory for as long as I can remember. In the nineteenth century, so the story goes, the town elders were given a choice between hosting West Virginia's state penitentiary or a soon-to-be-announced land grant university. These practical men, given the choice between free prison labor and a standing army of fuzzy-minded professors, leapt at the former. One is tempted to throw in "and the rest is history" here, but such historical determinism has its faults. There have since been too many possibilities at redemption for that choice to have dictated a destiny. And besides, the narrative is awfully clean cut, suspiciously so, even for that historical cliché. No, what makes the story so compelling is not its explanatory simplicity, or even whether it passes the smell test of truth, but rather that choosing a prison over a university is just the sort of thing that people where I come from would do.

Moundsville, West Virginia, lies on the east bank of the Ohio River, just a short barge and tugboat ride downstream from Pittsburgh. We drink the Steel City's wastewater and brownfield runoff, in fact. This forgotten outpost of boarded-up smelters and steel mills lies just beyond the Pittsburgh Metropolitan Statistical Area per "the Feds," as we liked to call them while playing Cowboys and Indians. (Even at a tender age, we usually identified with the Indians.) It does not matter much to us where we technically belong. Reality prevails here. Of the variety of industrial manufacturers that once lined the river before the economic apocalypse of the early 1980s, all that remain are the anus end of some coal mines, paint plants, and a few chemical manufacturers, which yield products similar to those which caused a disaster in Bhopal, India.

To be working-class in Moundsville was to be truly on the bottom of the slag heap of society. Shunned by Pittsburghers and Clevelanders for its southerness, and by the rest of West Virginia for its sundry north-of-the-Mason-Dixon Catholicisms (mostly Italians and Eastern Europeans, with an occasional Greek thrown in), the northern panhandle of West Virginia can even shun itself. This was most recently witnessed when country music star and favorite son of Glen Dale (just north of Moundsville) Brad Paisley went on *Jay Leno* to defend his song "Accidental Racist," which is about how it has become unacceptable to wear a Confederate flag T-shirt. For the record, West Virginia entered the Union as a free state in 1863 and fought on the blue side. But most locals don't know that. Whenever this neurotic northern sliver of West Virginia is missing from CNN's crude election-night maps, moral outrage follows. Residents are flummoxed by assertions that this place does not in fact exist.

My ancestors were Asturian Spanish, stocky little human espresso machines who came to West Virginia from the silver-mining regions of the old country during the 1920s.

Their expertise in mining and smelting was in great demand. They lived in Spanish Row's squat matchbox-like houses, in a little bastion of papism and domestic violence located down the street from the constant *clink-hum* of the Pepsi bottling plant. The matchbox simile is not imprecise. Inside these matchbox houses were little hotheaded match people who threatened to explode with self-destructive violence if rubbed the wrong way.

Pepsi was the official non-alcoholic drink of Spanish Row, the bottling plant having been owned by one of its enterprising residents. The Asturians in my family shrub were too proud to sign anti-anarchist and communist statements at Ellis Island, and subsequently redirected to Cuba to mellow out a bit. They made it through Ellis Island in a more amenable state of mind a few babies later. Lured by posters offering mining work in West Virginia, they wound their way through the Alleghenies and northern Appalachians, carrying their stubborn, erect postures into the heart of darkness. Photos show them in tight, cruel shoes and starched collars, staring uncomfortably into the flash of the camera. They were known to abuse cats.

The Asturianos, too proud to refer to themselves as Spaniards, did not take well to the local customs, I am told, or rather the locals did not take well to them. Holed up at the windowless Peso Club down the street from Spanish Row, the Asturianos organized labor after being fired as prison guards for agitation. It was at the Peso that I had my first Pepsi out of a frosty mug pulled from a horizontal deep freezer by a thin guy attired in an impeccable white undershirt. The Peso was cold, winter cold, like the frosty mug, the coldest place I had ever been during the summer. The

Asturianos back in Spain, the stay-at-home Monteses and Zapicos, became legendary anti-fascist fighters in the 1930s. Some lived on in exile in Paris as late as the 1990s. I tell their story knowing I am attempting to make identity lemonade out of identity lemons.

From the employment of my grandfather to my junior high school education, the penal colony on Jefferson Avenue, the State Pen, played a greater role in my life than anyone will ever know. My junior high school was overrun by the progeny of inmates from all over the state seeking proximity to Dad's weekend visitation. These violent miscreants, challenged in basic hygiene, were promptly labeled "dirt balls" and considered genetically predisposed to all sorts of degenerate acts in the restrooms and locker rooms. They played a central role in our needy psyche: they were people we could look down on.

When I first heard the term "Rust Belt" during my last year of junior high, the rust had barely formed on Moundsville. I immediately assumed this rust belt was a reference to the local repurposing of a fashion accessory as a disciplinary device, a tactic that increased in response to the stresses of rapid deindustrialization. Childhood infractions small and large were reacted to all the same: the belt was released by grimy mill hands, swung with cracking precision, and re-sheathed between frayed belt loops, all in a matter of seconds. The Ohio Valley in the early 1980s was marked by patterns: for every mill closure, bankers closed in on the houses, women dried their eyes with pink Kleenexes, and the belts came off. Then families moved away or fell apart.

I have always wondered whether Moundsville suffers under a curse. The mammoth stone-walled penitentiary we called the "butt hut" was ruled unfit for even prisoner habitation. It was repurposed as a federally funded SWAT team training facility, until it was discovered that the mock explosions were releasing unsafe levels of asbestos. The corrections facility moved to the outskirts of town, in the foothills off a road called Fork Ridge.

Across the street from the abandoned butt hut, the city's namesake, sixty-nine-foot-tall Grave Creek Mound stands like a big green earthen tit. The Adena mound-building civilization populated this region between 1000 and 200 B.C., or "before the curse," as we said in school. Our mound is thought to have been built near the end of this period. Early Moundsvillean, amateur archaeologist, and tomb raider Delf Norona dug exploratory shafts into the mound in 1838 and exhumed bodies. Thus we speculate a curse not unlike that of Chief Cornstalk's curse in downstream Point Pleasant, West Virginia, which local lore claims as the backstory behind *The Mothman Prophecies*.

There is a distinct possibility that I have personally contributed to Moundsville's curse. Of many nights spent drinking cheap regional beer on the peak of this venerable structure, one evening stands out in particular.

The late-summer evening was cool, but tired, with the feel that it was finishing off a muggy day. The chill blew off the river as I met up with Chet and Greg at the shopping plaza. We stood around smoking cigarettes, bored and feeling taller than we were. The idea came to Chet to buy a case of beer, but as none of us had ever drunk any, we weren't sure just how one went about it. Our back was to the drink

mart. We talked ourselves into the notion that this purchase should be like any other. We pooled our discretionary
income. It came to $8.50, just enough for two six-packs of
Rolling Rock and some beef jerky or a case of Iron City
Light. We chose the latter. Nobody was hungry.

Chet, an honor student like the rest of us, was a dreamer,
unable to focus on anything. His drunken old man railed at
him every morning until Chet agreed to pull the lawn
mower from the shed in the alleyway and canvass the neighborhood for work. He found plenty. The first half of the
summer went by rather uneventfully, until one day Chet
was distracted by some flight of fancy and allowed the
mower to roll backward over one foot. With a dull thud and
the sound of cracking bone, the mower stalled. A large toe,
covered in wet grass clippings, landed on the sidewalk.
Without that toe, Chet walked with a slight limp. It didn't
seem to bother him.

We made our way past signs for the impressive-sounding
Grave Creek Mound Archeological Complex. One of us suggested drinking right there. We turned in unison and looked
up at the mound, knowing full well that the only place worth
drinking on this property was at the heights. Greg and I
hoisted our sacramental offerings over the green chain-link
fence to Chet, who waited on the other side. We carried the
beer up the spiraling stone stairwell to the statue at the
mound's peak. The sun was setting behind the ComEd coal-
fired power plant across the river, rendering the horizontally
blown white smoke in hues of red and orange. Horizontal
exhaust meant clear days ahead, the smokestack serving as a
sort of primitive Weather Channel. Two blinking jets on the
way to somewhere very different from Moundsville left puffy

contrails in the sky. The red sunset bounced off the muddy water below, giving the image of a river on fire.

We plopped down on a stone wall and just stared at each other silently before Chet popped open the first beer. Greg and I followed suit and all three of us grimaced at the taste. The cold Iron City Light stung with an unfamiliar bitterness, something like a blend of tonic water and gasoline.

From the peak of the mound we had a clear view over the penitentiary walls. What I had thought was one gargantuan building in my youth was actually a massive four-story wall, as thick as a car is wide. Inside was a complex of buildings, an open-air hell. It was a mysterious place occupied by murderers and child rapists, eerie long before it was closed down and turned into a place for freak tours and Halloween haunts. Criminal silhouettes danced on frosted windowpanes.

Stories abounded about the pen. Like the guy who was burned alive by gasoline in his cell during a riot, or the warden with a German name and knee-high leather boots who would challenge prisoners to fights after removing his badge.

Chet turned around and commented on the glow of the sunset. We turned around with him, and then we saw it. A truck jacked up to a ridiculous height bounced down the street, pitching and yawing with each seam in the road surface. Oversize exhaust pipes jutted vertically out of the truck's bed. The driver slouched in the seat, with his right hand low on the steering wheel near his dick and his left arm leaning on the door. His female passenger sat at his side, snuggled close on the bench seat, à la mode at that time. As the truck rounded a corner, the driver leaned his head out of the window and released a dark stream of chewing-tobacco juice in a manner only made possible by dental peculiarities.

"High-altitude hillbilly," Greg blurted out. The spitting driver was no doubt one of the ridge-running locals who found his identity in southern West Virginia, while Chet was the type who looked northward along the industrial riverfront for his. On this mound we straddled the fault line of two cultures.

"A good case for forced sterilization," said Greg ruefully. He was back on his forced-sterilization soapbox again, a theme he had beaten to death that summer. Greg had thoroughly absorbed—to its dangerous conclusion—the elitist mind-set of the gifted program's lead teacher, who flaunted a doctorate in education from the state university that Moundsville had passed up.

"Actually, if you want to sterilize people, you could start here," insisted Greg, pointing epiphanically toward the penitentiary, which by now was lit up brighter than a Steelers game on *Monday Night Football*. A guard was visible in a Gothic-style turret, looking around with binoculars during what must have been a shift change. He turned in our direction. I thought about my grandfather, who died decades before my birth, climbing that same guard tower and perusing the grounds with his binoculars. The houses on the hills surrounding the town stared darkly like pillboxes.

"You can't just sterilize people," said Chet. "They are still people."

Chet and Greg's friendship had been strained since the Betrayal, when Greg chose to play on the laughingstock football team rather than play trumpet in the state-champion marching band. It was an unexpected move, given Greg's complete lack of sports experience and his three years in the junior high band. He wasn't athletic, he was just big. He would play defense.

The acrimony between the band and the football team was the most talked about conflict in the town, after the inevitable union-management conflicts. The band made the team seem like an appendage of a music show. It was safe to say that most spectators turned out to watch the band, and not the football games already given up for lost. The coach and band director were no longer on speaking terms. The band entered the field at the same time as the team, which more than once led to a smashed tuba or broken bass drum. It seemed vaguely revolutionary at the time to see the football team as the side act surrounding the halftime music show. Later in life, when I had a greater appreciation for sports and a suspicion of military-influenced music, I came to see this was an omen that there was something wrong in our universe. Greg took a loud slurp from his beer and sat silently.

"What about Fred?" I asked. Fred was the elderly wash boy at the local Ford dealership. He had done some hard time for chopping up his wife and her lover with an ax. He had caught them in the act while returning home early one day. Fred, one of the few black men in town, became a sensation after his release, treated as a hero and given a $50 a day sinecure at the dealership. He mostly sat leaning against the doorjamb and picked his teeth with a Bic pen.

"Yeah, we can't sterilize Fred," said Chet. Greg had to concede the point. "Besides," added Chet, pointing to the penitentiary, "most of the people in there are in for life. They can't replicate their DNA anyway. You can't knock up a butt." Chet was proud of his use of the word "replicate."

Greg sat silently, unable to find a response. He took another slow slurp at his Iron City before smashing the can and throwing it down the side of the mound.

"Well, I'm just saying that it makes sense in theory," said Greg. "I'll admit that there are problems in practice . . . like Fred. That has to be sorted out. "

Greg had been reading Herodotus. He had found a dusty copy of the Greek historian's writings in a local library. Greg told us the story of a leader who had been toppled by an enemy force. The leader was forced to watch a procession of his family being marched off to death, but he only cried when he saw one of his servants in the procession. We sat for a while and debated why that could be, concluding that stories are more powerful when they lack clear explanations.

I stood thinking about the earthen protuberance on which we sat, thinking about all that had transpired since this dirt was piled upon bones upon dirt. Rome went on a conquering binge. Christ was crucified. The Jews were driven from Jerusalem. The Sassanid Empire rose in Iran, and Constantinople became the capital of the Eastern Roman Empire. The Vandals sacked Rome, and China was reunified under the Sui Dynasty. Muhammad died, Arabs seized Constantinople, Charlemagne was crowned Holy Roman Emperor. *The Tale of Genji* was written, the Crusades were crusaded, and Saladin reconquered Jerusalem. Genghis Khan croaked. The Hundred Years' War began and ended in about a hundred years. The Bible was translated into God's language of English, and America was "discovered." Jews were ejected from Spain, Copernicus wrote, and Bruno burned. The Ming Dynasty was formed, and the Gregorian calendar was adopted. Cromwell croaked, America revolted, the French revolted, Karl Marx,

the Bolsheviks, 20 million dead in World War II, gas cham-
bers, the atom split, Jews return to Palestine, Beatlemania
and the Ayatollah.

And now the civilization on this little speck of earth was
falling apart. But the mound would remain. And so would
the penitentiary, a testament to Moundsville's true work:
locking people up and desecrating the dead. Everything
around us was changing except the stars in the sky. Under
that postcard-picture sunset stood the fragile, naked life of
our drunken bodies.

LAYLA MEILLIER

Love and Survival
A Flint Romance

I COULD NOT APPRECIATE WHAT Flint had taught me until I let myself fall in love. For years I dodged it; I could not even commit to a favorite color or TV show, let alone a person. When you're not in love you can never be hurt in such a vulnerable way. As a young woman, I don't blame this city for my lack of puppy love; I blame this city for my fear of feeling vulnerable.

My first love was a bike. A sleek hunk of purple pipe with sparkly wheels and handlebars. I collaged my bike in goofy stickers I had begged my mom to buy me at Rite-Aid one day. I was not permitted to leave my neighborhood, but I did not mind because my world seemed vast.

At the time, we lived on Mountain Avenue in the College Cultural neighborhood, a place in the city considered more suburban without a too-safe uniformity. Homes range in size and era of origin, and the people tend to the unique and artsy. They look out for one another. In other words, it's a go-to spot for young couples moving to Flint with extra money. The house we had was a brick duplex that looked like a German cottage. My stepdad owned a glass company in the north end that has long since been closed down. In its day, the company did well. There is never a scarcity of broken glass in Flint.

Although I was told time and time again to put my bike in our door-less garage behind the house each night before bed, one night, like ya do, I forgot. I left the nose of my bike barely peeking out from behind the house. To my naive surprise, someone took it in the night.

The news of this evoked a sadness I was not familiar with at the age of ten. At ten, one cries easily, pouts easily, sobs easily, but I could not make a sound. I felt as though my eyes had turned to stone and I wished I could not see out of them. My parents told me about the theft in an awkward family meeting, standing in our cramped kitchen. They filled me in on the normalcy of this sort of situation in my hometown: "There is nothing we can do. The police are too busy with other things. This happens all the time."

I went to my bedroom in a haze. A week went by and I didn't even go outside to play; instead, I took to throwing weird shit down our dumbwaiters and retrieving it in the basement laundry hamper.

Then, one day, my bike was back!

"They found it," was all I was told by my numbly shocked mother.

Years later, I was hanging out with my now ex-stepdad, catching up around the holidays, and he was feeling a little toasty. "I lied to you that time when we were living on Mountain," he said.

"What?"

"I lied about your bike."

"What do you mean? What happened to my bike?"

"The police never found it."

"Yes, they did; it was my bike . . ."

"Yeah, but I found it. Not the police." I stared at him in shock as he unfolded the tale of how he happened to be driving in his big company truck through the east side one day, looking for a house that needed an estimate pre-installation of new glass, and he noticed a yard that was "covered in colorful kid shit." He figured he'd check it out. Lo and behold, my bike was among the mismatched wreckage. He planned to confront the people living there, a reasonable goal for a man of his size, covered in intimidating tattoos.

"I found your bike, laying on its side on the ground."

"Those bastards," I said. I never let my bike lay on the ground; I always used my kickstand.

"Yeah, right, the bastards! So I stole the bike back."

"What? In the middle of the day?"

"Yup. I went and knocked on the door but no one came. So I just took it. I slid it in my glass rack and took off."

I needed some time to process this before I asked, "Why didn't you ever tell me?"

"Well, because I never wanted you to think stealing back was the answer and I guess I didn't want you to feel like the police can never help you."

Fair enough. Either way, since that day, I've been paranoid about my stuff. I don't feel so bad about losing things as having them exposed. I would rather my belongings be reasonably lost and safe than displayed. When I was a preteen and spent time walking around the city alone, I wore baggy clothing. I stuffed my hair up in a neutral cap but never put my hood up—with it up I can never see my peripherals—unless I felt terribly angsty that day, like I didn't care if someone snuck up behind me. *Don't leave your stuff out; don't be a female; don't wear pastels; don't fall in love.* It was all too painfully vulnerable. Until one day, years into my aged-cheese adolescence, it hit me, while I was lying in bed with my lover.

He was sleeping and I was not. I watched him for a few minutes, closed his jaw when it popped open and stank morning breath burned my eyes. I put my face real close up to his and pretended time had stopped in the moment just before a kiss and we were frozen. And then I got that feeling, like before when I should have been crying but I couldn't and my eyeballs turned to stone. I realized he wasn't vulnerable because I did not want to hurt him. I was taking ownership of my vulnerability and forgetting the dependence vulnerability has on external forces. What about trust? If you are trusting, you are vulnerable . . . but will external forces feel more inclined to hurt you if you trust them? No. Is life about always putting your bike safely in the garage? No.

I don't typically wear my heart on my sleeve but when others need it, I leave it peeking out from behind the house and let them take it for a week.

It's easy to get let down by this city and get angry and look at everyone on the street like they might have to fight you, but that just creates more problems. I'm still here because the lessons are complicated and I want more than anything just to learn how to be a good human being, to be vulnerable, and to love.

Day to Day in the Rust Belt

A Middle-Aged Student's Guide to Social Work

JOHN COMES INTO THE MAIN office of the community outreach and says, "I've been in fucking jail all fucking week," then dings the bell sitting on the receptionist's desk, even though the receptionist is right there, eating a mint and doing a crossword puzzle like she always does on Fridays when she volunteers.

I'm behind a cubicle wall, on the phone with a woman who needs two months' rental assistance. She talks, then sometimes stops talking to sigh or groan. The desperation in her voice makes her sound like she's stuck in an alley and the man with a gun in her face is her landlord. I listen. I acknowledge. I take notes. She calms but I'm as distant as a 911 call.

She says, "It just happened," meaning how she went broke.

I understand broke.

I understand the speed at which it happens.

John says, "Fucking jail."

He says, "All fucking week."

I'm new here. This is February. I started my field placement in October. Six months before this, I'd never heard of a field placement. Jobs people worked for experience and college credits—but not money—were called internships. I was too old for an internship. I was too old to be a student getting a master's degree in social work. In December I turned forty. I had a wife and two kids, whom I loved dearly, whom I seldom saw now that I was a middle-aged student with an unpaid internship and a bunch of random facts on notecards I needed to memorize for a bunch of upcoming tests. A year before this I'd taught writing full-time at a university, an always unstable job doled out in yearly contracts, until I was released with a letter that said, basically, "Nice work, no thanks." Before that I'd taught classes at another university for part-time wages and without benefits. I'd published one novel. Another novel was about to be published. For years, for decades, I'd built my life around writing and teaching. I wrote because I loved to write and I taught because I loved to teach writing and I needed to make a living and I'd assumed I could make a living from teaching, especially because I worked so hard as a writer when so many of my colleagues did not write or publish at all.

Then, like every other job in America, it was gone.

John says, "Five days in jail, not fucking good."

Phone on my ear, I lean out from behind my cubicle to make sure it's John, and it is, I knew it from his voice, part cough, part thirst, the night before and the morning after, rain and sun and snow and leaves, a desperate combination of his vices and the seasons he toughs through to make a living. I wave but he doesn't see me. He stares at something on the wall, some poster someone in the community has put up, offering services, rides to and from the doctor.

Sue, the receptionist, faces me. She looks scared. John can

be intimidating, even when he hasn't been in jail. I hold up my finger: *one second*. I slide my chair back to my cubicle.

The woman on the phone is very sweet, despite her desperation. She needs at least one thousand dollars, two months' rent, plus she's behind on her utilities. I have the blue intake form in front of me. It still looks new sometimes, confusing, even though I've been using the form for months. When I'm busy, especially when two or three or four people all need help at the same time, the blue intake form looks like a page in the Bible, tiny rules I can never keep straight.

Last week, I forgot to get a man's zip code. There's a line on the blue intake form, an inch long, maybe shorter, and I missed it. I wrote nothing. The man talked. I listened. I wrote other things, things not zip codes, as he offered them or after I asked a question. I knew his income. I knew his religion. I knew his phone number. I knew he had kids and a church, but not where he lived, not exactly, not the zip code, just the house, just the flooded basement, just the landlord taping notes on his front door saying he was going to slap on a padlock. I told this man I would talk to my boss. I told him I would call him back, that I thought we could help.

I took the blue intake form and went to my boss.

"What's his zip?" my boss said.

My boss knows the form, taught me the form.

I said, "Shit."

I called the man back. The man said his landlord was at the door, banging. He was taping a note. He was threatening the padlock. I asked where he lived. I could hear the landlord's fist on the front door, knuckles on wood. It sounded like a hammer.

The man said, "McKees Rocks."

I said, "What's the zip down there?"

He said, "One-five-one-three-six."

I said, "I'll call you right back."

Back in another cubicle, my boss's cubicle, I repeated the numbers off the blue intake form and my boss said, "Out of our service area."

I said, "We can't do anything?"

My boss said, "Tell him to call the United Way."

"The United Way?" I said.

This is part of the process—if you can't help someone, you refer them to another organization, another nonprofit, another charity, a church, even, which may or may not be able to help them or which may refer them to another organization that may help or may keep the referrals going until the person who needs help circles back to the original organization but days later and with even direr circumstances and less money and more people looking to collect. Or this person may just fall. It goes: shelter, homeless, dead.

My boss—kindhearted, easy to work for—is used to this. I'm not.

More people come for help than we can help. Who gets help is a confusing process for everyone: the people who need help and the people who help. The money is not enough—the grants, the donations, none of it. One set of numbers means assistance. Another set does not. I can seldom remember the numbers because the numbers are illogical or bogus or impractical or unnecessary or simply a figure to show government officials and voters who confuse poor with being lazy. The poor have become shadows—they're here always but only visible in the darkness under bright light and sometimes look like nightmares.

If I go to the roof, right here in Bellevue, on top of the old Allegheny General Hospital, where our office is located, where they generously rent us three rooms for a dollar, where we sweat all day because we share space with the boiler room and it's always ninety degrees, even in winter—if I leave the heat and take an elevator and stand on the roof above the fifth floor, I can see McKees Rocks, right there beneath the bridge, right before the tunnels. I can see the houses and the old rusted-out mills and the machine shops where no one works anymore. I could drive there in minutes. I could run there. I could fall right over the bridge and land in the dirty water.

Out of our service area, my boss said.

We are here, and they are there.

I want everywhere to be in our service area, even though I know that is impossible, even though I know it would be worse, that we wouldn't do anyone any good.

McKees Rocks is an old mill town, the kind of place that lost jobs when all the steel mills moved away. I knew a guy, years ago, who used to score blow in an old house near a tattoo parlor, down by the river. I think the tattoo parlor is still there. I don't know what happened to the guy who used to do blow—maybe dead, maybe quit, maybe a lawyer, maybe still at home on his mom's couch. All those people I used to do drugs with when I was a kid and young man seem like characters I know from books, from movies, all of them stuck in time. It's hard to imagine someone who snorted coke in a bathroom stall with a Budweiser bottle balanced perfectly on his head ever growing up, let alone old, but I was there, too, waiting for my line.

The world forgives worse.

But then, other times, the world doesn't forgive anything at all.

I tell the woman on the phone I will call her back. The blue intake form is complete. I have her zip code, the wrong numbers, but still. I tell her that the most we ever give for rental assistance is five hundred dollars. I give her some phone numbers to try and drum up the rest of the money. I will, later, call those places for her myself. I do not tell her she is out of our service area because I want to find a way to put her in our service area. I think there are exceptionally bright people, talented people, math people, who know how to do this but they work elsewhere at organizations that are not nonprofits and they do not work for college credits or for free.

But right now, we have John, just out of jail, not happy about it.

I come from behind my cubicle and say, "Hey John, I thought that was your voice."

John slumps in a chair. There are four chairs crammed into this tiny space we jokingly call a lobby. Three fans swish the hot air around so it cures our eyes like meat.

John says, "Hey Dave," and nods like he's defeated, like jail and everything else have already won. John wears a green winter coat. He is not, inexplicably, sweating.

I look at Sue.

Sue says, "Dave, this is John. John is here to see you."

Sue is sometimes a beat off.

Six years ago, she was diagnosed with multiple sclerosis. A year later, she quit her job at a bank because she couldn't stand for long hours and started volunteering here as a receptionist two days a week. Sue walks with a cane. She has a loud laugh that makes people uncomfortable. She sometimes screws up basic tasks, transferring calls, taking messages. Everyone in the office thinks Sue is deteriorating. They think it's the MS. It may be. But I think it's us. I think we make Sue nervous and conscious of her MS and she starts thinking about her MS and her cane and the way one of her legs drags slightly and how we notice it and she forgets to think about what she's doing, transferring a phone call, taking a note. I've taken to screwing up in front of Sue on purpose. I drop things and lose pens and ask where forms are. Some days, there is enough time to screw up on purpose and still recover. There are minutes and hours when the phone doesn't ring and people don't come in asking for free food and free bus tickets to get to work. Last week I knocked over a candy bowl and crawled around on the floor, looking for Jolly Ranchers, and Sue and I laughed all afternoon at my clumsiness.

Sue says, "John is just out of jail."

I say, "I thought I heard him say that."

John says, "It is just unfuckingbelievable."

"Jail, or that you're out?" I say, trying to make a joke.

I've joked with John before. He's a funny guy when he's not just out of jail, when he's not feeling hopeless, when he has a job and some scratch.

I can't remember when that was exactly.

John showed up at the outreach in October, right after I started, when I wore confusion like a name tag. I'd been told what the outreach did by a couple different managers at a couple different offices but it felt too scattered and disconnected. We did food and rent and utilities and gave away winter coats and children's toys at Christmastime and other things, too: cheap cars for individuals slightly above the poverty level; Easter baskets and Giant Eagle gift cards for other people, at other distances from the poverty level. Mostly I sat at a desk, waiting. I read a bunch of pamphlets, but it all felt like PR, like good publicity. I wanted to talk to people, to clients, to anyone in need so I could find out what exactly we provided.

Once I spent an hour talking to a delusional man about the U.S. Navy and what they owed him in benefits and back pay for not allowing him to enlist forty years ago. I thought we could provide him nothing, not medicine and not therapy, but I loaded up three bags with groceries and we walked to his car weighed down with enough food to fill his cabinets. As for the navy, I suggested they weren't worth his time. They were impossible with back pay, especially for people they'd already jacked around about enlisting. It would be better to get in touch with his caseworker again; that woman would know where to find him some money to help with his rent and those people would be better than anyone on a boat or dressed up like an admiral, you could trust a caseworker; and so we talked until he calmed and drove off.

Delusions are not only for the delusional.

If you expect anything, even the chance for your own dirt, you lose.

John stares at his hands, two pink cracked babies. He wants to talk but everything you say when you've been in jail is not what you're supposed to say. He mostly "motherfuck"s.

I'd read two books on narrative therapy before I started back to school. Narrative therapy asks: Are you telling your stories or are your stories telling you? If you're only telling the worst about yourself in the worst possible way then you need to find a way to change your story, to focus on the strengths, to find a story that includes the best parts of your life.

It's like in *Hamlet*: *For there is nothing either good or bad, but thinking makes it so.*

If you say your life is shit, it's shit.

I'm making this sound simple but I think simplicity is where to go. In the next two years I'll take class after class on therapy after therapy, and each therapy will desperately detail itself into sounding different from the previous therapy by citing some statistics and some scientific tics, like conversation is the same as penicillin, like helping someone get out of bed who is too depressed to get out of bed is open-heart surgery. I believe people need to talk. I believe other people need to listen and, when necessary, talk back. People who don't have money will always need money. That's why I got into social work: to talk to people who don't have money and to help them get whatever they need.

John needed money when he came in the office back in October. His truck was out of gas, stuck on the side of the road. His tools were in his truck. Without his tools, he couldn't work. Without work, he couldn't pay the bills. The story was telling John in the worst way.

John is in his mid-fifties. He's worked construction for almost forty years. He looks it. The damage on his face is everywhere: lines, creases, bumps, scars, moles, dark blotches, fresh cuts. His teeth are yellow from cigarettes. His fingers are yellow from cigarettes. His eyes are sometimes as red as Mars. He's skinny and muscular and walks with a limp.

"I been chasing disasters my whole life," John said.

We were in the lobby on that day, too. My boss was busy, working on a grant. She asked if I wanted to try to do an intake. She gave me the clipboard and the blue form. I gave it to John. He filled it out and handed it back and started talking.

The last disaster he chased was Hurricane Katrina. He'd been working in Florida when the storm hit, so he packed up his tools and headed west. Disasters brought work and big money. In Florida, John had mostly been drinking. A couple times he'd been on landscaping crews, just to make some dough under the table. Two weeks into New Orleans, John had a grand stuffed in an old toolbox he kept locked away in his truck. A week later, it was fifteen hundred, and he was living good, eating meat and drinking whiskey.

"Not rotgut," John said. "You drink?"

"I drink," I said.

I wasn't sure if I was allowed to say I drank. The outreach was not a religious organization but they had religious ties. I tried to imagine myself as John's therapist—how much distance was necessary? How much professionalism? How many boundaries? How much honesty? I decided to go with honesty.

John said, "Whiskey?"

I said, "Mostly beer."

"A lot?"

"Sometimes."

John went back to his story. He worked for one guy in New Orleans but there were other guys, other contractors, everywhere. This other guy offered more money, a lump sum for two months' work. John took the job. He started gutting old houses, pulling the copper wire. He did that for a while. He breathed in a lot of mold but didn't worry about it. The foreman moved John outside and up a ladder to the roof, where he nailed shingles with a gun. Then he was inside, doing plaster. John loved to plaster. "It's my master trade," he said. All his clothes have paint and spackle on them, rips in the knees and elbows. He wears painter hats. A smudged-up rainbow is dripped across his boots.

While John worked on walls, he didn't get paid. He lived on the money he'd stashed in his toolbox. That was fine. He slowed down on the whiskey. He started eating out less. He started eating peanut butter right from the jar for dinner, sometimes dipping the knife in jelly. He expected a check for ten grand, more if there was a bonus. There were sometimes bonuses at these kinds of jobs, at these disasters. Two months went by. John didn't get paid. The contractor said one more week. Then two. John said sure. He stayed on. The contractor asked for another week. Then he upped it again. They were talking four weeks now, three months instead of two.

The price went to fifteen grand. John was going to be fucking rich.

Then the contractor was gone.

The contractor was gone with the crew of guys he brought with him from Seattle and the rest of the guys, guys like John, wondered how they were going to pay the rent at their shitbird motel.

"I was fucking angry," John said. "I was going to kill that motherfucker."

John planned to drive to Seattle to rattle that contractor's head with a hammer but the more he thought about it

the more he felt confused. Maybe the contractor said Portland. Maybe it was Tacoma. Everywhere up there sounded
the same, green and wet and cold.

One night, drunk, John used his hammer to smash up his
motel room instead. The woman running the motel called her
boyfriend and her boyfriend, a huge biker, told John he would
either pay for the damages or go to jail. John paid for the damages. He paid five hundred dollars, even though he could have
fixed the walls for the price of spackle and some paint.

That's when the depression set in.

Those were John's words.

"That's when the depression set in," he said.

Earlier I said that John was funny, implying he wasn't always depressed, but John has always been depressed. He's
always depressed, only some days it doesn't sound like depression because it's mixed with jokes and stories, sad jokes and
stories, but still jokes and stories. John asks questions. If he
talks too much about himself, he digs deeper and refocuses
and asks about you, about your troubles. But his troubles are
still there. Every conversation has a moment where he asks, "I
wonder if it's even worth it?" and I ask him if he's serious, if he
wants to go somewhere, to a hospital, to talk to someone, and
he says, "No, I'm still hanging on pretty good." He always
says, "I'm fine, just depressed."

I'd heard of the *DSM*, the book doctors and mental
health workers use to diagnose disorders, but I hadn't
bought a copy until graduate school. Depression, like so
many other disorders, was still a vague idea, a thing from
books and TV, from films, from people on the street, people
singing to themselves with dead eyes. My grandfather had
been diagnosed—by a doctor, not a book—with schizo-

phrenia in the 1950s, and I knew he heard voices, I knew he thought he was Jesus sometimes, and Jim Plunkett, quarterback for the Oakland Raiders, other times, but I'd never read anything about it. Doctors told my grandmother and my grandmother told my dad and, years later, when my grandfather came to visit, my dad told us, his children, that our grandfather was not quite right. When John told me he was depressed, I thought: Hell yeah, you're depressed, some guy just screwed you for fifteen grand.

But later, when I open the *DSM* for the first time, there will be John. I'll read the criteria for Major Depressive Episode, and it will be like reading John's biography.

John is depressed all day, every day.

John is not interested in anything, even TV.

He will say, "I drink whiskey, and I don't even like the taste."

He will say, "I don't even like getting drunk."

He will say, "Peanut butter don't even taste good."

He won't be eating. He will be skinny, wirier every time he comes around. He won't be able to sleep because he's so worried about work. He'll feel too tired to look for a job. He'll feel like he's fucked up everything in his life. He'll feel like it's his fault that the guy in New Orleans drove off with all his hard-earned money.

John will say, "I'm ashamed to ask for help."

He will say, "I wonder if it's even worth it?"

"It's worth it," I will tell him.

That first day I talked to my boss about John, she gave me three Giant Eagle gift cards and I handed the cards over in an envelope. John bought warm food from the deli, mac and cheese and fried chicken, and he used one card for gas. He filled up his truck and drove back to the apartment he was sharing with four other adults, a couple of middle-aged guys who chased disasters like John did, and their girl-friends.

John started coming to pantry. Pantry was a food bank but we called it pantry because it sounded better than canned vegetables and ramen noodles. Pantry was packed but I always asked John how it was going, what he was up to. Work was scarce, he said, but he'd been doing stuff for a temp agency. He said he was on a crew. I could feel how proud he was to have a job, to be pulling himself from the muck. I walked him to his car. We shook on it, on everything. A week later, he showed up in the morning looking for emergency food. He was struggling. He was broke. He was broke even though he still held the same job on the same crew. "These fucking temp jobs," he said.

That crew was going somewhere in a pickup truck when the driver took a bend too fast and John rolled from the truck bed and shattered his arm on the asphalt. He held up the cast. Everything from the wrist to elbow was metal. The next time we talked, it was worse. His body was rejecting the pins and screws. His arm was yellow. Then the arm stabilized. Then the doctor said John would never work again, that he was fully disabled. John said, "I worked my whole fucking life." Then John had a lawyer and was suing the temp agency.

Now he's in our office, just out of jail.

The temp agency said they would settle and promised checks but the checks haven't arrived. John is completely broke, which is broker than broke, broker than before. Last

Friday, someone, a friend, sort of a friend, a guy John recognized from the neighborhood, offered to buy drinks at the bar if John would drive. John drove. The cops stopped him on the way home. They asked him to exit the car. They asked him to walk a line. They took him to jail.

John says, "That was five days ago."

I say, "That was seven days ago."

John says, "It's Friday?"

I nod.

John says, "I'm going to jump off the fucking bridge and break my neck and drown."

"Don't do that," I say.

It's the first time I've ever heard John articulate exactly how he wants to die, how he's going to do it. I look around the office and feel the dry heat blowing in and think about what I'm doing and what I'm supposed to do. Social workers have a code of ethics. Those ethics say you cannot let a person walk off and die. I ask John if he's serious. He says he doesn't know. I ask him if he wants to go to the hospital. I tell him they will help him at the hospital. There are doctors. They have beds and food and people to talk to.

John says, "I don't got insurance. I don't have a way to get to the nut hospital. They impounded my truck and I can't afford to get it out."

I say, "I can drive you," and I will but I don't know if I'm allowed to.

I don't know the outreach's policy about taking clients places. Everyone who works here is a woman and they don't like to be alone with the male clients, who are generally few but loud and frustrated and angry. Last year, one guy threw a can of creamed corn through a window at the food pantry.

Another guy smokes weed in the bathroom and denies it while laughing. Another guy seizes and collapses to the floor and is too big to be lifted.

John says, "I really only came in here to see if you have some clothes." He flares out his winter coat and lifts his shirt and shows off the waist of his jeans. The jeans don't have belt loops and they buckle on the side. He says, "They're women's jeans. The jail lost my clothes and this is all they had. It's like a bad joke."

"They look good on you," I say.

John smiles a little.

I think sometimes I'd like to be in charge of a charity organization so I could make all the rules then change the rules to whatever I need the rules to be. I'd run my charity organization with a bat. I'd knock on the doors of temp agencies and poverty-wage employers and universities who charge students to work jobs and call them internships and I'd show my bat and I'd say, "Honestly, what the fuck are you doing?"

I think about that then ask John what he wants, what he needs.

He says, "Jeans," and laughs.

I ask him if he needs any food. He asks if we have any peanut butter. I tell him we do. We have peanut butter but it's in a cabinet and, for some reason, we are not supposed to give it out. The peanut butter stays in the cabinet, even when people want—no, need—peanut butter.

I leave John and go to the pantry and go in the cabinet I'm not supposed to go in. The cabinet is full. All the shelves are full. I fill up three bags with groceries, lots of bread and peanut butter and jelly, and bring them back to John.

He says, "I can't carry those," and he lifts his arm, his

helpless arm, like a tiny bird without wings trying to fly from his shoulder and getting stuck and falling down to his lap.

I tell John I'll take him home. I tell him to wait and I go back and ask my boss if I can take John home. She says she wouldn't but I can. I tell her I want to. I walk around to the front of the hospital and find my car. I load in the groceries and pick up John at the back door.

He says, "Thanks for this."

I say, "Not a problem."

We drive over the bridge and down below us is McKees Rocks. A famous boxer is from there. I can't remember his name. Billy Mays, the TV guy, the guy who used to be in all the infomercials, the guy who pitched OxiClean, the guy in a blue denim shirt with a nice beard, the guy with the great voice, grew up in the Rocks. When he died, when his heart exploded from years of cocaine abuse, it was all over the national news. Billy Mays. Pittsburgh. Heart attack. Cocaine. But not John, he never makes the national news. Construction, ripped off, broken arm, hungry, depressed. They don't loop that on CNN.

But now John has groceries and we are driving, driving and talking.

Years ago, when I was twenty-two or twenty-three, I started to read Walt Whitman and I found these lines in one of his poems: "Despise riches, give alms to every one that asks." He said, "Stand up for the stupid and crazy, devote your income and labor to others." He said, "Hate tyrants, argue not concerning God." Whitman was a poet but he was also a nurse in the civil war.

He said, "Have patience and indulgence toward the people." He said, "Take off your hat to nothing known or unknown or to any man or number of men." He said, "Go freely with powerful uneducated persons and with the young and with the mothers of families."

He said, "Devote your income and labor to others."

He said, "Stand up."

My brain aches sometimes from how much I want to be better, from how often I fail.

John and I drive to his apartment. The bricks of his apartment are yellow, some crumbling, some no longer present so there are open spaces and dusty concrete. I park out front but he doesn't get out. He leans on his door. He sighs. I lean on my door. He wants to talk and I want to listen. He wants to talk about bridges and jumping from them, and he does, naming bridges, naming heights, until he wants to talk about other things, better things, small things, steaks, hamburgers, french fries, New Orleans, about the food down there, fried fish, fried clams, fried shrimp, about sandwiches and cold beers. We do that until we circle back to bridges and jumping and falling and dying and how bad that would be, to die before his settlement arrives, to die before he can prove those fucking doctors wrong, before he can work again, before he can build something again, or at least paint it, something, some job, any job, some kind of work because he can still do work, he doesn't need an arm, he doesn't need a hand, he could paint a room with a brush in his teeth, and then John's like *fuck bridges*, and I'm like *fuck bridges*, and he's like *fuck death*, and I'm like *exactly, no death, no dying, not now*, and John promises me he won't kill himself, and we shake on it, we are men who love to shake, and he promises to make a sandwich, because if you're going to be alive you have to eat, you have to make a sandwich, maybe not a po'boy, maybe not shrimp, but something, you need to start somewhere, you start with food.

I carry in John's groceries. I wave hello to his roommates, all adults older than me, dressed worse than me, looking more exhausted than me, all happy to see John, all moving to the kitchen to see what John has brought, to see what's in the bag.

Outside the sun hides behind the trees, and I have kids at home, and a wife, and so much homework, so much homework I do not want to do.

I start my junky car and I am starved.

ERIC WOODYARD

Fresh to Death

TAY STEPPED INTO ARLENE'S NIGHTCLUB fresh to death on a chilly Sunday night in October.

He was clean as hell, rocking a pair of flashy True Religion jeans and burgundy Bally sneakers, with a tan sweater trimmed in matching burgundy. The words "Trouble Man" were stamped across his chest.

A flock of fine-ass chicks trailed his smooth cologne scent. From the outside looking in, he was a true baller.

He mostly stood near the bar, with his homie Duke, sending shot after shot to the loosest females in the building. By the end of the night, he was setting up a play for the baddest of them all.

Duke and Tay were the local promoters of the comedy show happening at Arlene's. Ciroc Boi Entertainment was their official tag.

Tay was my brother. We weren't related by blood, but Tay was truly like family to me. He was a devoted father, son, brother, hustler, and a certified mack. You'd rarely ever catch him stepping out to a club or bar and not looking fly—even if he was just popping in for a split second. He grew up down the street, near both of my grandmothers on the nutty north

side of town. I met him so early in life that I really can't remember any formal introduction. His aura reminded me of
that of legendary boxing champion Floyd Mayweather, with
his slight stutter and bright smile. Tay could light up any
room.

I had a lot of love for that dude, and whenever we stepped
out together I was guaranteed to have a fun time. But on
the night of the comedy show I was chilling at my mom's
house because my body had shut down from excessive alco-
hol consumption throughout the week. I'll leave it at that. I
needed to get my black ass mentally prepared for work the
next morning and I couldn't take a chance at partying too
hard with Tay that night.

Duke and Tay had flown in a comedian from Washington, DC, as the headline act, and even with a modest crowd,
the show still had to go on.

Unfortunately, the bulk of the folks—looking to drink
and party—didn't arrive until after the comedian's set had
already ended. But Tay and Duke still showed the comedian love and blessed him with a portion of their earnings
from the door. Tay kept the jokester's cup filled with vodka
shots, too. Shit was all good.

By 2:00 A.M. the countless Cîroc shots and Bud Ice
started to kick in.

Everybody at Arlene's was feeling a good buzz as they
headed for the door. Tay and Duke even lined up a few chicks
to come home with them, but there was one problem: the
liquor store was closed.

As the owners shut down Arlene's, Tay and Duke were
among the last ones to leave.

Tay skirted off recklessly. He punched at least sixty miles

per hour on the dashboard down North Saginaw Street in his white 2007 Dodge Charger. Tay was headed to an after-hours spot to grab another fifth of Cîroc. Duke took off in the opposite direction in his green truck to get gas before entertaining the women.

Wandering closely near the door of the after-hours spot were a couple of strange-looking black dudes, according to an eyewitness whom I promised would stay anonymous. One was tall and light-skinned and the other was a muscular, dark-skinned guy with a thick beard.

Tay knocked on the door then gave the guys dap as he waited to get in.

"Wassup, my nigga!" Tay greeted them.

"Are they charging in there, my nigga?" one asked.

"Probably a couple of dollars, if that," Tay said. "You just gotta buy some drinks."

"Man, I ain't buying no drinks," the other guy said. "Is they searching?"

"Yeah, they're gonna pat you down or something," Tay explained as they walked back toward the door.

As he banged on the door again, the light-skinned guy exposed a handgun.

"You know what man run that shit," he told Tay.

"Y'all niggas are gonna try to rob me?" Tay asked.

"Run that motherfucking shit before I kill you," he repeated.

Tay placed his hands on the door with a gun pointed toward his head as the dark-skinned guy ran his pockets.

"That's fucked up that y'all niggas robbing me like this." Tay shook his head in disbelief.

"Shut the fuck up before I pop you," the tall guy yelled.

Tay beat on the door again before it finally flew open. He ran in, explained the situation, and raced back out to spot the thieves. The duo was still in the same spot. As soon as the robbers saw Tay coming back out, they fired.

Tay's body collapsed on the hard concrete as soon as the bullet entered his left temple. A stream of blood flowed from his head onto the street as paramedics arrived on the scene. His clothes were soaked in blood.

"Oh my God, Tay!" a woman screamed. "Talk to me!"

He never recovered. Two days later, on October 22, 2013, at Hurley Medical Center, Tay took his last breath. He was thirty-two years old. The news hit me like a shock wave.

I'll never forget that day. I was lying in bed, chilling with my pregnant girlfriend, when my mother barged in the room to deliver the news.

"Tay just died!" she yelled.

I jumped out of bed in disbelief. Tay and I had been hanging out that entire week in celebration of my twenty-fifth birthday. In fact, I was right at that same after-hours spot that he got shot in front of just four days before the incident.

What if I had decided to attend that comedy show with him that Sunday night? I would've likely trailed him to get a bottle of liquor. Would those guys have shot me, too? Maybe I wouldn't be here, either. That's a scary thought but a truthful one. To make matters worse, Tay's girlfriend was also pregnant with his daughter. He couldn't wait to father his third child. We discussed fatherhood that entire week.

"Can you believe that this gonna be my first baby that I'll be out of the joint to raise from day one?" Tay kept saying, smiling. "That shit crazy."

"It's gonna be wild," I said, as we passed around a bottle

of Cîroc. "Our babies will be tight since they're so close in age."

"I know," he told me. "If it's a boy, I'm gonna name him after me, but if it's a girl her name will be Dessiah."

Tay never got a chance to even learn the baby's gender. Maybe someday I can tell Dessiah how cool her daddy was.

Moving on the streets of Flint in the late night can be deadly. It took my losing Tay to really grasp this. In the daytime, many people identify me as Eric Woodyard, award-winning sports reporter, but at night people see me differently. There was once a time where I partied nearly every night. In fact, I still like to go out but I'm way more cautious of my surroundings.

Stepping in any club around Flint, especially the hood ones, you have to be prepared to encounter some bullshit. It's really that serious. Anything can break out.

That tension hangs in the air to this day. It's a weird line that I have to walk—between downtown corporate Flint and where I was raised; between night and day; between the two different identities I've formed. There's that side of me that likes to live on the edge and then there's the responsible father that excels in his career. To keep it plain and simple, I try to resolve that tension by using Tay as an example of when I feel that I'm going overboard.

Growing up in the Fifth Ward of Flint, there weren't many places around town where I didn't feel comfortable. When you aren't bothering anybody or involved in illegal activity, why would you be afraid of going anywhere? But in Flint, trouble can still manage to find you if you're in the wrong place at the wrong time.

Tay was like me. He went out a lot. He drank lots of liquor. He messed around with women. Life was fun for Tay. He lived single and carefree.

I still remember walking into the newsroom the next day after Tay was shot. Somehow, I kept my composure and didn't mention it to anyone on the job for fear of them asking me to connect a reporter with the family. That was way too far beyond my comfort zone, to assist anyone with sources for that. The headline on the article written by one of my close coworkers read: "One man in critical condition after shooting at Flint bar, suspect in custody." Later in the week it was updated to: "Man dies after being shot outside Flint nightclub." To them, Tay's death was just one of fifty-two homicides in 2013. Four more folks were murdered after him in the city that year. Flint's death toll was actually at its lowest since 2009, but all it takes is to lose one person and the statistics go out of the window.

As sad as it was for me and my family to lose Tay to senseless violence, it also taught me a valuable lesson.

Sometimes life isn't fair and when it's your time to go then it's your time. You can't beat death. Tay wasn't bothering anybody when those guys gunned him down. Being fresh to death in Flint could literally be your cause of death.

Rest in peace, Deonta Blackmon.

Rust Belt Heroin Chic

SUMMER 2014

At the far end of the West End meeting room there's an old
disco ball hanging above the coffeepot. The meeting that's
about to start is listed as one about alcoholism, but maybe
half the people in attendance are recovering heroin addicts,
many of them from halfway houses and renewal programs.
A few kids sit at folding tables, puffing on e-cigarettes and
vapes. Little clouds of mist rise toward the ceiling fan. When
I got sober in 2005, you could smoke in there. The walls are
still stained nicotine-yellow.

SPRING 2009

When you're involved in a custody case in Allegheny County,
one of the first requirements is parenting class. The class
Gracie's mom and I are assigned takes place in an East End
elementary school—a gray stone building with a fenced-in
playground. Before class starts, I stand in the shade with my
coffee, smoking a cigarette. Across the street, kids play home
run derby with a metal bat and tennis ball. It smells like last
night's rain.

Inside there's a projector and a bunch of tables set up in the cafeteria. I grab a pamphlet and sit. Seats fill slowly. No one says much. Jane shows up in sweatpants, stuffing a half-smoked Newport back into her pack. She sits next to me and smiles as if I were a friend she just ran into at the supermarket.

Class will run for two hours with a break in the middle.

We watch a slide show that teaches such salient points as: Don't hit your child, don't hit your co-parent, don't fight in front of your child. Get your child to school every day. Feed your child every day. Bathe your child. Do not use drugs around your child.

At break, when I go outside to smoke, the shade is gone and so are the kids playing ball. Jane looks high, but I probably do, too. My eyes itch and they have dark circles beneath them. Jane pulls the half-smoked Newport from her pack and asks me for my lighter, which I hand over and stare at until she's finished lighting her cigarette and I motion for it back. She tells me she can't afford court. I tell her I don't care.

AUGUST 2009

When I start graduate school, Gracie stays with me two nights a week. I have three night classes and two dinner shifts at the restaurant. I'm living in Avalon.

My lawyer tells me calling Children and Youth Services is a last resort. Avoid confrontation, he says. Write everything down.

I make lists on envelopes and use them as bookmarks.

FALL 2009

Jane is six hours late for agreed drop-off time.

Jane is two hours early for agreed drop-off time.

Jane asks for money for diapers. I bring diapers to her grandma's house. She already has diapers.

Jane says she needs money for gas to get to her shift at Eat 'n' Park. I put gas in her car.

Later, I stop by Eat 'n' Park, and the manager tells me she was fired months ago. I get pie and coffee.

SUMMER 2014

Outside the meeting room, in the lobby, there's a vending machine and a Big Buck Hunter video game. The woman behind the counter is wearing a T-shirt with wolves on it and an ankle bracelet with a blinking green light. She gives me a coffee, I drop a dollar in the tip jar and look around to see if any of my friends made it down. Past the vending machine there's a chalkboard where people write the names of recovering addicts and alcoholics who have died, details of the funeral arrangements, and upcoming NA dances.

The previous winter, fentanyl-laced heroin called "Theraflu" led to a rash of overdoses. Close to thirty people died in a week. Recovering addicts spoke in meetings about how they wanted to go out and shoot the dope that was killing everyone. Newspapers ran stories of kids dying and think pieces on the heroin crisis. The stories mentioned the initial flood of prescription drugs, the government regulations and resulting rise in prices. Suburban kids who'd gotten hooked on Grandma's cancer meds started going to the North Side for $10 bags of dope rather than shell out $80 a pill for

Oxycontin. In 2006, the killer heroin was called "Get High or Die Trying." The same thing happened then.

I ask a buddy of mine, a recovering addict, about fentanyl and heroin. "Fentanyl is a painkiller, like twenty times stronger than morphine. A lot of heroin is cut with it," he tells me, "but if the cut isn't right, you can get a bag that's mostly fentanyl. If that happens, when you shoot it, you'll probably die."

I never shot heroin. I drank. At my worst, I might black out after three drinks or twenty. I had auditory hallucinations. I drank in the morning. I shook. I puked. I fought. I treated everyone in my life like garbage, and lost almost everything. But I played it all up as part of being a writer. Great effort I put into living like some kind of Kerouac wannabe, so I could write about all the wild shit I did. Toward the end, I barely left my apartment. I barely wrote.

OCTOBER–NOVEMBER 2009

Jane moved out of her grandmother's house and into an apartment with her friend Lisa in Perrysville.

Lisa and Jane's apartment is one-bedroom. There are two dogs. Smells like weed and piss.

Fridge is full of crab legs and German chocolate cake.

Stopped by Jane's apartment after work, around eleven, with table scraps for the dogs. No one was there. Jane's phone went straight to voicemail.

My lawyer files an emergency motion to remove Gracie from the apartment in Perrysville. Gracie stays with me until Jane moves in with her mom, and we start sharing custody again.

DECEMBER 2009

Jane is hospitalized after crashing her car at 3:00 A.M. Gracie was home sleeping. Her mother didn't know Jane had left.

Jane's mother lives in Evan's City, a small town in Butler County. Both *The Crazies* and *Night of the Living Dead* were filmed there. About a week after the car accident, I head up for Gracie's Christmas pageant. I step into the church basement, holding the puzzle I wrapped in the parking lot. Inside, I see Jane with a bag of frozen vegetables pressed against her cheek, sitting at a card table, drinking cider from a straw. I sit across from her, and she takes away the bag. One eye won't open, the other is dark red. Blue stitches cross her face like rivers.

Jane says, "I fell asleep at the wheel." She adjusts the bag. "I could have died."

I pick at the cracked tabletop under the blinking Christmas lights. There's a row of staples behind her ear, down along her jawline. I ask what happened.

"I was at a meeting," she says. "We went for coffee after."

"And you fell asleep at the wheel."

Jane sets down the bag and raises her voice. "Why are you being so mean?"

The room goes quiet. I fight the urge to go out for a smoke and instead shuffle over to the tree and put the puzzle with the other gifts. Everyone eases back into conversations about the Steelers.

I grab a coffee and head upstairs for the pageant.

The camera on my phone won't work, so I try to commit it to memory: my two-year-old daughter with a tinfoil halo, wisps of hair in her eyes. Her voice is soft, almost hoarse. "Joseph," she says, "we've got good news."

Two pews over, Jane starts crying, says, "They grow up so fast." Her family consoles her. They all take pictures.

For the finale, the class sings "Jingle Bells."

Coffee and cookies afterward while Santa passes out gifts.

A woman from the church gives Jane a ham.

Still wearing her halo, Gracie hovers at my knees. The rings under her eyes are as dark as mine. "Mommy hurt her face, but she'll be better soon," she says. "Me and Gram prayed while she was at the doctor."

I pull her shoulder close to my hip.

"Daddy, I don't like Santa."

"I don't either."

"Hold me."

I lift Gracie up, she grabs my neck, and I watch her mother.

By Easter she'll be bloated and strung-out. But right now she's as thin as the branches scraping against the stained glass. Jane pulls the bag from her face, and a circle of parents step back when she shows off her scars. That sky-blue thread holding everything together.

SUMMER 2014

In the meeting room, I sit in the corner by the door so I can leave if anyone starts talking about Jesus. The lights are dim. Next to me there's a pile of donated clothes on a fold-ing table. I stare at the holes in the lace of a skimpy night-gown, while someone shares about gratitude or God, or maybe triggers.

As the hour passes I hear stories: a stolen car traded for $20 worth of heroin. Gold teeth pulled out with pliers to pay for crack that turned out to be fake. Months spent in a condemned house in McKees Rocks, high on meth, tortur-ing a dog chained up in the basement. Kicking dope in the back of a van. Copping psych meds in Shadyside when the insurance runs out.

In the opposite corner of the room, by the literature rack, there's a new girl chewing on her shirt sleeve. She fidgets in her chair and stares at the chipped tile floor. The preppy kid in the teal polo shirt sitting next to her gets up for coffee twice in ten minutes then leaves for the bathroom. When the meeting started, they said they came right from rehab.

FEBRUARY/MARCH 2010

Jane's mom tells me Jane failed a home drug test.

Jane's mom kicks her out of the house.

Jane moves back in with her grandmother.

SPRING 2010

Jane's getting lazy. She doesn't even bother to smear makeup over her track marks anymore. The lies get more outrageous; she contradicts herself midsentence sometimes. One night she drops off Gracie, asks to use the bathroom and runs the shower for half an hour. Says she's waxing when I knock. I wait, knock again. When she doesn't answer, I open up the door and she's asleep on the toilet. Cigarette turning to ash in her fingers, steam fogging up the mirror. Leg wax like puddles of honey on the bathroom floor. Strips of pale skin on her legs. I go through her purse and find stamp bags and needles. I turn off the shower. She comes to and I confront her and she starts sobbing.

"I need help. Don't take Gracie away." Jane tries to hug me. I step back.

She has no one to take her to detox. She's too fucked up to drive. I can tell she's stuck between wanting to get indignant over me looking in her purse and the fact that she's guilty. Guilt I can't imagine. And she knows that I know she's been lying to me for years even though she'll refer to it later as a "slip." Like, she just had that one little slip where she got high for five years after she'd been clean for seven. No big deal. One day at a time. But for the grace of God. Et cetera.

Gracie is watching Tinker Bell in the living room, in her pajamas.

"Your mom has a really bad headache," I say. "I'm taking her to the doctor. You're going to stay with Gram. You'll have so much fun."

"Okay, Dad. Is Mom okay?"

"Yes. She just needs to go to the doctor. For her headache."

I take Gracie to her grandmother's and head to Mercy Hospital. On the way, I stop outside a house in Perrysville and give Jane ten bucks to cop a couple Xanax.

I drop Jane off at Mercy. On my way home, Jane calls. They don't have a bed for her. I stop at my place, hide my few valuables. Then I pick up Jane, and she spends the night detoxing in my bedroom. I fall asleep downstairs in front of the TV.

Two days later, we go to the Suboxone clinic in Monroeville. None of the places that will take her insurance can see her without an appointment. The office is like something from a Vonnegut story. There's New Age music playing, incense burning. Motivational posters on the walls. Miniwaterfalls flow over decorative rock gardens in the waiting room. The well-manicured male receptionist talks like a telemarketer and smiles too much. While Jane deals with the doctors, I take Gracie outside. We sit in the grass island between the strip mall and the office, and toss a plastic ball back and forth while the nurses take their smoke breaks by the Dumpster. Then I pay for Jane's Suboxone, and we leave.

Jane refuses to go to rehab, but the new custody order states I can request Jane be drug tested, and that she must live with another adult for Gracie to stay overnight. Unless I can prove Jane is causing Gracie physical harm, or is under the influence while she is in her care, I can't get full custody.

FALL 2010

My second year of grad school starts, and I spend my loan overages on another retainer for my lawyer. I move to Bloomfield. I start teaching creative writing in the Allegheny County Jail. I'm assigned the women's class. My students who have children miss them dearly, but I can't sympathize the way I think I'm supposed to. Maybe two of them aren't in on drug-related charges. Their stories are all so similar. Stories like Jane's. A woman is born into poverty.

Subjected to domestic abuse from parents and stepparents and partners. She finds heroin or crack or both. A way to cope, maybe. Then comes the crime in support of the habit, but she can hustle, at least for a while, but it gets to be too much. Maybe, she thinks, having a child will help. She'll have a new purpose, someone to love her unconditionally, but when the son or daughter comes, it gets worse. Maybe her man leaves and her family won't have her, and there's a familiar way to cope but she can't hustle like she used to. Then maybe the state takes the kid to be brought up in the system, ready to repeat the cycle.

Sometimes during class, I wonder what I have in common with the men in my students' lives. In Jane's version of her story, I'm the bad guy. I'm the one who wouldn't take her back when I found out she was pregnant, and now I'm trying to take her child. I make fun of her father going blind from MS in the hills by State College. Call her every name you can imagine. Tell her Gracie would be better off if she'd hurry up and overdose and die. Get it over with already so we can move on with our lives. I become self-righteous and indignant. But I hate myself for the position I've put my child in. I hate myself for hating her mother. For being too scared to take Gracie and skip town. And so many of the beautiful moments I spend with my daughter during the first four years of her life are experienced under a cloud of constant worry and self-loathing.

SPRING 2011

Jane's friend Lisa goes to inpatient after getting caught with stolen goods and heroin.

I finish grad school.

Lisa gets out of rehab, overdoses, and dies.

SUMMER 2011

When I show up to get Gracie, she's crying on the front steps. "I don't want to go. Daddy, why are you taking me away from Mom?"

"Honey, it's our time to have fun together. Let's get ice cream."

Jane steps in. She speaks in an affected, baby-talk voice. "Gracie, I don't want you to go, but your dad says you have to."

Gracie cries, "No."

Jane says, "These are the rules."

The stress is going to break me. I write and work and raise a child, while Jane collects welfare and gets high. Why can't I get high? Drink myself blind and come to behind a bar in western Maryland, covered in piss and dirt, left to piece together the night before using hand stamps and bruises.

Jane buckles Gracie into her car seat and closes the door. Jane and I are standing outside of the car. Pink scars twitch across the bridge of her nose.

I say, "You've been strung out for three years, and it's my fault you don't get to see your kid more."

"We both just have today."

"You have track marks on your hands."

"You're harassing me. I'll call the police."

"Good. Call them. Please."

"Don't argue in front of my daughter."

When I get in the car to leave, Jane runs behind me so I can't back up.

At least Gracie isn't crying anymore. She's sitting in her car seat playing with her fairies. "Daddy, what's Mommy doing?"

"I don't know, sweetie."

I try to pull ahead through the side yard onto the cross street. Jane runs in front me.

I get out. "You're insane."

"You're not taking my daughter." She runs up and shoves me. I put my hands above my head in surrender.

Jane screams, "Don't put your hands on me," and shoves me.

"Get out of the fucking way," I say. And I wonder what it would feel like to punch Jane square in the face. Feel her glasses break and her nose explode. Blood on my knuckles, getting stuck under my nails. I'd wind up in county jail, maybe in the writing class I used to teach. Maybe I'd talk to some MFA student about how much I miss my kid while he praises my work for its realness. Get it all on the page. Write through the pain. My life would be over. I'd see Gracie for two hours a month in some Lysol-smelling room in a building in Penn Hills with a social worker taking notes, while we play with worn toys on a bald gray carpet.

I keep my hands up.

Jane hits me in the chest. Then her eighty-seven-year-old grandfather hobbles outside. "Don't you touch her." Grandpa picks up a rake.

This is what my life has become. My drug-addled baby's mom and her rake-wielding, arthritic grandfather, attacking me on their front lawn.

Back in the car, I inch forward, like I'm going to cut through the yard. When Jane tries to get in front of me, I whip it into reverse and drive backward out the driveway and down the street. Jane sprints after the car.

"Daddy, what's Mom doing?"

"Exercising."

We get out of the development, drive a few miles. Flashing lights spin in the rearview. I pull over. A cop comes to the window, carrying a stuffed moose.

He says my name like it's a question. *Please step out of the car.*

The cop opens the back door and hands Gracie the moose. She says thank you, looks curiously at the doll, then drops it on the seat next to her.

I get out of the car and explain the situation as best I can.

FEBRUARY 2012

At a Rite-Aid near Hampton, Jane is arrested and charged with shoplifting, possession of a controlled substance, paraphernalia, and child endangerment.

Jane pleads to misdemeanor possession of prescription drugs. I don't find out about the charges until the following summer.

I enroll Gracie in kindergarten at a magnet school in the city.

AUGUST 2012

A month before the start of the school year, Jane tells me she signed Gracie up for another year of preschool in Shaler. She claims I never told her about kindergarten.

I have to go to court just to get my five-year-old daughter into school.

The judge rules Gracie will go to kindergarten in the city. A new custody schedule is set: a fifty-fifty split.

When Gracie stays with me, we go mini-golfing. We color and play cards and have tea parties. I let her draw on our apartment walls and they're still covered in seven years' worth of stars and trees and clouds of every color. Phrases from children's songs she writes in her loopy block lettering. For a while, I have a modicum of normalcy and routine. Gracie is happy. Kindergarten comes easy for her.

HALLOWEEN 2012

Gracie is inside dressed as a fairy, playing with her aunt. Jane is nodding out on the front steps. I walk up the driveway. "You are fucked up."

"It's my medication."

Her eyes close and she burns her pants with a cigarette. "Wake up. You're falling over."

NOVEMBER 2012

Jane checks herself into rehab.

I tell Gracie her mom went away to school for a month, and will be back soon. Jane writes Gracie heartbreaking letters that I'll probably never show anyone.

After rehab, Jane moves into a halfway house for single mothers. Fridays, I pick up Gracie from school and we drive to the group home in Carrick. "Mom has roommates now. Tell me if any of them are ever not nice to you, okay?"

"Okay, Dad. Love you, Dad."

On Saturday nights, Gracie stays with her grandmother. She stays with me Sunday night through the end of the school week.

FEBRUARY 2013

Jane leaves the halfway house early, and ODs in the bathroom at her mother's house. She lives. I don't find out about the overdose until almost a year later.

Jane moves back in with her grandmother.

Everything is calm until November. When I get a Facebook message from this guy Steve, an ex of Jane's, who goes on a rant about Jane getting high and all kinds of shit I wish I didn't have to take seriously. He keeps asking to buy me lunch in Butler. I decline. I tell Jane she needs to take another drug test. For the first time, she doesn't argue about it. She pisses clean.

SUMMER 2014

Someone is sharing about gratitude or God or triggers. With fifteen minutes left in the meeting, the kid in the teal polo shirt comes back from the bathroom and sits down next to the jittery girl he met in rehab. He leans over and kisses her on the mouth. Then he turns bluish gray and falls to the floor in the middle of the meeting. It is the only time I've seen someone overdose.

I go outside and smoke while the woman working the counter comes in and shoots the kid full of whatever that stuff is you're supposed to shoot junkies full of when they OD.

It took getting sober for heroin to affect my life.

I met Jane in 2006, outside the meeting room with the disco ball where they're trying to pump life back into that poor fucking kid. An ambulance arrives. I get out of the way.

PRESENT DAY

Technically, Jane is still not allowed to be alone with Gracie.

It took months after getting out of the halfway house, but Jane eventually got her shit together. As far as I know she's been clean for over a year. In many ways, she's a great mother. She figured out Gracie needed glasses and got her eyes tested. I thought she just liked sitting too close to the TV.

Gracie and I still have our weekday routine. The roughest times are Sunday nights, when Gracie first leaves her mom.

I put Gracie to bed, and she says, "I miss Mommy when I'm not with her. Is it okay if I cry? I can't stop the tears."

I hug her and I tell her of course it is.

There's nothing I can do to stop them either.

*Author's note: All names have been changed, but everything else is true to memory.

Will Blacks Rise or Be Forgotten in the New Buffalo?

IN BLACK NEIGHBORHOODS SCATTERED ACROSS Buffalo's East Side, residents must be wondering what all this Buffalo Happy Talk is about. Buffalo is not a happy city for most of them. It never has been. When black folks look around Buffalo, they see the city being re-created for whites: college-educated millennials, the creative classes, refined, middle-aged urbanites, and retired suburbanites.

As a black historian and urban planner, looking through a glass darkly, I can see Buffalo rising. Yet, I can't help but wonder for whom the city ascends. If you visit Buffalo's so-called hot spots—Harbor Center, the waterfront, Allentown, the Elmwood Strip, Chippewa Street, and the Theatre District—you will see mostly hipster, latte-drinking whites. When you visit those neighborhoods where housing prices are rising and where swank rental apartments are found, you will find the same hipster, latte-drinking whites living there. Even in upscale apartments, like the Bethune and Elk Terminal lofts, which are located in the black community, you will find latte drinkers.

Yeah. I hear the rhetoric. The new buzz words are "equity," "inclusiveness," and "diversity." For example, Greater

Buffalo's regional plan, "One Region Forward," states, "Woven throughout the planning framework are two critical issues that define where we've been and where we want to go—our relationship to our fresh water resources and our desire to grow our economy in a way that is *more equitable* [emphasis added] and locally rooted."

Yet, I am troubled.

I can't stop thinking about that old African proverb, "What a person does speaks so loudly that I cannot hear what they say."

I believe that Black Buffalo will be marginalized in the rising city, just as it was in the shrinking city and in the prosperous industrial city. The plight of Black Buffalo has never been important to Buffalo's leaders. At every stage in the city's history, black neighborhood development has been an afterthought in city building. Buffalo and its Erie County suburbs were never meant to nurture and provide a healthy place for blacks or Latinos to live.

In the 1930s, when Buffalo leaders imagined a new metropolis—a combined city and suburbs—it was designed as a place for white, higher-paid workers and the professional classes. The most desirable housing and neighborhoods in the city and suburbs were reserved for them. These places enabled whites to obtain the highest-paying jobs, the most desirable recreational areas, and the best education, health care, and police services. In their fancy, segregated neighborhoods, whites lived longer, healthier, and happier lives than their black, Latino, and immigrant cohorts. My friend Carl Nightingale, the University at Buffalo historian, says this segregated world was the consequence of political action, not economic realities or simple racial hatred.

Don't get caught up in this race hatred thing.

This was mostly about white privilege; it was about whites using the neighborhood edge to get the economic and higher-standard-of-living edge. This was about whites being given an advantage over blacks, which was rooted in the economic organization of the city. Whites did not get this socioeconomic edge by accident or simple merit. They had help. City leaders consciously and deliberately designed an urban metropolis anchored by mass homeownership, race-based suburbanization, and neighborhoods stratified by housing cost and type. Whites were empowered to use guaranteed Federal Housing Administration (FHA) loans to purchase homes in the suburbs or along the city's leafy West Side parkways and avenues.

Blacks, meanwhile, rented in the grimy East Side. To keep them there, Buffalo's leaders used urban planning, zoning laws, building codes, subdivision regulations, and eminent domain. They forced blacks to live in houses situated in the shadows of factories, railroads, and commercial establishments. These were the worst places to live in Buffalo and Erie County. The racist FHA gave money to whites, but denied blacks access to home-buying dollars. And when blacks did manage to get mortgages, the location of their neighborhoods caused housing values to fall rather than to rise. For them, homeownership produced debt, not wealth. African Americans were stuck in place.

Whites and blacks experienced metropolitan Buffalo differently.

The 1950s and 1960s were the most dynamic period in metro Buffalo's history. Whites and blacks experienced it differently. Thousands of whites moved to the suburbs, where they found the American Dream. Blacks, on the other hand, found the American Nightmare. As thousands of black newcomers poured into Buffalo City, the urban bulldozer roared through their neighborhoods, destroying homes, playgrounds, churches, shops, stores, and fraternal organizations in its wake.

Black neighborhoods were collateral damage in the remaking of Buffalo and Erie County. Remaking the city and suburbs meant that black neighborhoods had to be knocked down to make way for downtown expansion, institutional development, interstate highway connectors, and wider roads. These "unbuilding" activities merged with plant closings and out-migration to hit the East Side with sledgehammer force. This urban disfiguring process left the East Side with miles of vacant lots and empty structures; it's a physical setting so scarred and foreboding that Robert M. Silverman, University at Buffalo urban planner, has called it Zombieland[3]. Today, the most distressed and blighted properties in Erie County are found in this part of Buffalo.

The mutilation of the East Side is not benign.

It robs people of the value of their homes. An East Side homeowner said to me, "Dr. Taylor, the house next door to me is empty, with a tree growing through the roof. It is worth sixteen thousand dollars. My house is in good condition, and I have big investments in it; and it is only worth eighteen thousand dollars. I don't get it. I'm still going to put another twenty thousand dollars into my house, even though I know I will never recoup it. So, I am making this investment in my

---

[3] http://www.thecyberhood.net/documents/papers/dawn.pdf

family and my children." This is how housing market dynamics operate on the mutilated East Side.

Cities don't grow like weeds.

The city's shape and form are the result of political decisions, not the invisible hand of economic determinism. Yesterday, Buffalo was built for white higher-paid workers, professionals, and business elites. Today, the city is being built for the white creative classes, or the latte group, as I call them. This is a broad group of whites, including folks in the arts, educators, researchers, doctors, and other professionals. To make them happy, urban leaders are refashioning the city with hipster neighborhoods, recreational areas, and public spaces where the latte group can converse, bike, jog, work out, attend outdoor concerts, and congregate in restaurants, bars, and coffee shops. The latte group bathes itself in liberalism and issues a clarion call for diversity and social justice, while simultaneously condemning the black and Latino masses to a blighted and disfigured urban dystopia.

The hard-core reality is that Buffalo's latte city, when stripped of its fanciful color-blind mask, is nothing more than a neoliberal white city—a place where millennials and the creative class claim the most hedonic houses and neighborhoods for themselves, where they live longer, healthier, happier, and more prosperous lives than Buffalonians of color, who are forced to live in the most undesirable and unhealthiest neighborhoods in the metropolis.

Black Buffalo is invisible.

Black Buffalo is Ralph Ellison's *Invisible Man*. Whites see blacks, but not really. Whites hear blacks, but not really. In preparation for a presentation at a recent forum on blight in New York state, I read numerous reports and newspaper articles on blight in metropolitan Buffalo, and the terms "black" and "African American" were rarely, if ever, mentioned. For example, even though blight concentration is synonymous with the East Side black community, Blueprint Buffalo, an action plan for reclaiming vacant land, said, "At the beginning of the 21st century, Buffalo has an unprecedented opportunity to identify, assemble, and reclaim vacant parcels for start-up businesses, new families, artists, entrepreneurs, and major commercial partners to join in the region's renaissance." Most of that vacant land is on the East Side, but there was not a word about black neighborhood development. There was not a word about urban leaders uniting with the black masses to transform and change the East Side.

Not a single word.

In the 2015 "One Region Forward" report on housing and neighborhood strategies, the challenges facing the black community are barely discussed, except in a veiled language that suggests ". . . for areas where disinvestment has left few of the assets, anchors and actors that are needed to power successful neighborhood revitalization . . . the time for conventional neighborhood development might be decades away." The authors never use the terms "black" or "East Side," but any person knowledgeable of Buffalo understands the code, and knows they are talking about the East Side black community.

My point is city leaders know about the challenges facing Black Buffalo, but they constantly feign ignorance and surprise. But they know. More than two decades ago, I teamed up with a group of scholars to produce the most comprehensive study of Black Buffalo ever undertaken. This blueprint for change, written by a team of scholars from the University at Buffalo, Buffalo State College, and Fordham University, along with support from the Buffalo Urban League and the City of Buffalo Common Council, was never implemented. Later, my center conducted an investigation of the health status of Black Buffalo, funded by Kaleida Health and the Black Leadership Forum. The study was celebrated and then put on a shelf.

In 2000, I led a team that outlined a strategy for the redevelopment of the east-side Fruit Belt community and demonstrated how tax increment financing could fund the plan. The study was funded by the City of Buffalo's Office of Strategic Planning. City and medical campus leaders praised the report, ignored its findings, and then launched their own redevelopment strategy, which displaced 65 percent of the Fruit Belt population.

Yes, Buffalo is rising and happy talk abounds; simultaneously, thousands of blacks are being displaced from their traditional neighborhoods along Main Street. They are being pushed out of every neighborhood of opportunity in the city. But no one seems to care or notice. Black Buffalo is invisible. Black needs, hopes, and desires are systemically ignored; promises are made, but never kept.

Yeah. I know some white person in Amherst is saying, "But Mayor Byron Brown is black. I don't get it."

Let's be clear. Black faces in high places don't mean a thing if they have the same agenda as white faces in high places. From a city-building perspective, the sad reality is there is no difference between Byron Brown, who's been in office for the past ten years, and Jimmy Griffin, who was mayor from 1978 to 1993.

Yeah, yeah. I know the mayor does hire more blacks and he makes better speeches than his predecessors, but his approach to city building still marginalizes and deems black neighborhood development unimportant.

It pains me to say this, but the mayor is fiddling while blacks are being displaced from neighborhood after neighborhood in Buffalo. He is fiddling while underdeveloped neighborhoods are spewing undesirable outcomes in housing, education, employment, and health. He is fiddling. The mayor knows about black suffering and pain, but the solutions to these nasty problems do not fit into the economic growth model he celebrates.

So black neighborhood development is chronically placed on the back burner. Yes, black faces in high places can support systemic structural racism.

But we, the people, have a choice. We have a right to the city.

Don't get me wrong. The white latte group moving back to Buffalo is a good thing. I get that; but the choice we face is not between the white hedonic latte city and blacks living in blighted, disfigured, and slum-like neighborhoods. *That's where the mayor gets it wrong.* The real choice, my friends, is between the hedonic latte city and the just city.

Hear me, Buffalo.

Our city does not belong to those powerful faces in high places; it does not belong to the developers, the bankers, and all those folks profiting off the latte city. We have a right to this city. The masses of black, brown, yellow, red, and white faces have a right to build the just city. We can make that choice. The future is "uncreated." It is not some type of preordained, futuristic place that is immutable and fixed. No! The future is "uncreated," and we have a right to build the just city, a good place, where we find liberation and the higher freedoms.

Buffalo! The time has come for us to answer Rabbi Hillel's question: If not us, who? And if not now, when?

AARON FOLEY

Can Detroit Save White People?

OKAY, SO, ALL YOU WHITE people coming from Brooklyn (or L.A., or Portland, or Austin, or Chicago, or London, or whatever) to Detroit looking to "save" yourself: What, exactly, are you saving yourself from?

I'm curious! What is it like being born into the most spoiled classes on the planet and wanting to move to a city full of black folks who have been ruined by centuries of your tyrannical rule? Serious question here.

All right, maybe that's being a little harsh. I didn't mean to call you folks spoiled. Because as we all know in New Detroit, we have to get along and pretend racism doesn't exist anymore. Just ignore all those elderly black people being pushed out of downtown. It's really just a class issue, don'tcha know.

What is this obsession? What is this desperate need for people to fix themselves in a city that's broken? You may heal, you may find your emotional center, but your surroundings remain the same.

Why is it that the Detroit I know is so drastically different from what all these starving artists think it is? The city that made me, that made us, who we are: driven to succeed, dressing to impress, never saying die, forever against the odds, is now becoming the Island of Misfit Toys? Is this your pilgrimage to Mecca? A journey through the universe to the softest place on earth? Who are you misguided strangers who aren't even close to having your life together in a city where we've constantly been told that we'd never be worth anything if we weren't on your level?

Yes, we were told that. Us east-side and west-side kids were always told to not even think about going to the parks in Grosse Pointe, to drive slow in West Bloomfield, to just ignore those stars and bars on the back of Taylor pickup trucks, and to outperform the kids in all the rest of the suburbs so that we might have a chance to get a scholarship to a U of M, an MSU or a CMU, only to be told on the first day of orientation that we were only there as pitiful affirmative-action cases and that our Detroit/Highland Park/Southfield/Inkster educations would never be enough to make it in the real world, so we go back home to make sure that the next generation would never have to deal with the kind of stuff we had to put up with, only now we have to deal with not only these overcrowded schools, these abandoned houses, these unpredictable summers, but on top of all this, these armies of confused Williamsburg rejects who simultaneously have all the answers on how to make it in Detroit after living here for five weeks but don't even know how to fix their own lives because they need to be "saved."

What are you looking for here that you can't find elsewhere? Can't you just admit that you came for the cheap rent? Because that's what it all boils down to, right? And that's fine. Perfectly fine, and I'm not being cynical or sarcastic. I love the fact that there are still places in Detroit that rent for the same as what my mom paid in Lafayette Park in the nineties. I don't love how the "cheap rent" excuse is fine for the newcomers but not the longtime business owners. But I've seen Brooklyn prices, and you'd be a fool not to take advantage of what we've got here. And we could certainly use more (live) bodies here. But can you at least be up front with your intent, and not cover it up with this hippie malarkey about "finding yourself"?

I'm not sure what else you're looking for, or what exactly you're trying to get away from when you say you want to save yourself. Again, save yourself from what? The unbearable guilt of feeling like a gentrifier, perhaps? Well, guess what? When you're moving here, that guilt will manifest in different ways. Sure, we've got plenty of empty space for you not to push anyone out because there's literally no one there. Telling people that your former hometown has "lost its sense of adventure," however, lends to this idea that Detroit is just your personal safari, filled with dangerous twists and turns and the unknowing of what will happen next.

That's the rub. That's what gets me, because we've lived here in Detroit all this time and we know how to get along here. But if I were to pack up and move to Montana tomorrow, of course I would be forced to grow up and mature a little and be prepared for the unknown, because I don't know where I am. I'm out of my comfort zone. And, just like the rest of you twenty- and thirtysomethings, I'm at an age where I really haven't figured things out yet, either. But that's the sort of thing that happens to all of us at that age, living in Detroit or not. Talking about Detroit in these wildlife terms is just as offensive as those of you on the opposite side doing all you can to erase the history—remember our "blank canvas" phase, everyone?—of the people that have been here. And, yeah, there's also that subtle undercurrent of racism when you talk about "adventure" in a city that's mostly black.

Why don't we just make a deal that when you move to Detroit, you just move here and shut up about it? Buy your abandoned building, build your lovely studio space and make art to your heart's content, but at the same time, keep that maudlin BS to a minimum. Get off this endless spiel of trying to "save yourself" and just pay some property taxes. Welcome to Detroit.

HUDA AL-MARASHI

Cleveland's Little Iraq

My husband and I moved to Cleveland from a high-rise in Queens with bewildered giddiness. In the mornings, we woke to the sounds of birds chirping. No sirens, no honks. Although the downtown was eerily quiet, traffic moved. Parking was ample, and the grocery stores' aisles were wide enough to accommodate carts with play cars attached—a dream come true for a mother of young children.

Still, I had my reservations about our new home in the Midwest. My husband and I were both the children of Iraqi immigrants. We'd moved to Cleveland for his work, and I didn't know how we'd fit in, in a region known for whiteness and farms. I doubted we'd find a Muslim community, let alone a Middle Eastern supermarket.

It only took me one trip along Lorain Road and West 117th to realize how wrongly I'd assumed. Those two streets boasted more Middle Eastern supermarkets than I'd ever had access to my entire life. During my childhood in a California tourist town, we made monthly hour-long drives to the closest Middle Eastern grocery. We came home with pounds of halal meat dumped into plastic bags that we then had to package and stack in the freezer. In New York, the scenario was the same, except I was the one with children underfoot as I portioned meat into freezer bags.

Now, only miles from my home, butchers prepared their halal meats in trays just like butchers prepared meats in mainstream grocery stores. They had a halal deli and frozen foods, fresh pita bread, and an assortment of cheeses, *lebne*, jams, and olives. I found the convenience of it all dizzying.

As I stocked my refrigerator at home, I told my husband we could live here forever. We mused as to where all these Arabs had come from and why we hadn't known there was a community here before. Maybe it was a spillover from Detroit? Maybe there were other Iraqis?

I discovered there were, in fact, many Arabs in Cleveland. At the Islamic Center of Cleveland—my first local mosque that actually looked like a mosque, complete with a gilded dome and minarets—I found Jordanians, Palestinians, and Syrians, but no Iraqis.

I didn't understand why I sought out this community. I hadn't been to Iraq since 1979, when I was two years old. During that trip, my parents were interrogated so intensely at the airport, they decided Iraq was changing for the worse and that it wasn't safe to return. There had been only a handful of other Iraqi families in my childhood seaside town, and in New York, the only foreign language I needed was the fragmented Spanish I used to communicate with my Colombian neighbors. I wished I could say that I missed speaking Arabic, but I didn't have that kind of relationship with my mother tongue. I had always been far more comfortable with English.

Still, I continued to search. At a Shia mosque in a converted church in Brecksville, we met Iranians, Pakistanis, and Afghanis. They were warm and welcoming, but I wished I'd met some Iraqis, just a few families whose dialect reminded me of home.

On our way out, an Iranian woman told me her neighbor was Iraqi and that she planned on attending the Eid al-Fitr party to celebrate the end of Ramadan. "Come," she said, "I will introduce you." Without my having to tell her, she understood what my young family needed: people who looked and sounded like our relatives, people who'd stand in as aunts and uncles, cousins, and grandparents.

At a west side recreation center, I met Lenna, the wife of a neurologist and the mother of three children. From her first lilting "Hellow," I knew Lenna was a real Iraqi, born and raised. Rather than introduce myself as an American who could barely speak Arabic, as was my habit, I had a radical thought: *Try.*

I surprised myself. By the end of our conversation, Lenna could tell Arabic was my second language, but still she complimented me, told me how well I spoke for someone born in the U.S. We exchanged numbers, and she introduced me to the other Iraqi families in the area, most of whom had immigrated in the 1990s after the first Gulf War.

I had found an Iraqi community without my mother translating for or obligating me, without my differentiating between Iraqis born in Iraq and those born in America. Those born abroad were my parents' friends—they loved gaudy furniture with gold trim, they arrived to everything at least an hour late, and they had little regard for posted rules (seat belts were optional. DO NOT ENTER signs were mere suggestions.). I befriended their children, who were like me—accent free, style conscious, and rule abiding.

In the company of my new friends in Cleveland, though, I discovered how many stereotypes I'd held of my own people. My notions of Iraqis were based on a single community, most of whom had immigrated in the 1970s, and much of what I'd observed had been generational. These women, however, were my peers, with similar interests and tastes. They dreamt of HGTV homes, arrived on time, dressed in the latest styles, and even if they didn't always wear their seat belts, at least they believed they should.

I became a full-fledged member of this new world. Now I was the one picking up the phone, inviting friends over, and being invited places. We broke our fasts together during Ramadan in apartment-building party rooms. We picnicked in parks in the summer. We chatted and ate as our children played. All year long, there were visits to be made for deaths, hospitalizations, and births that made the American in me rear her head at the endless socializing. But another part of me was proud. Every time I showed up with a cake in hand to welcome visiting relatives or to comfort those mourning the loss of a loved one was a small triumph over assimilation. My children would grow up knowing they belonged to more than just Cleveland; they were one more generation with ties to a country they'd never seen, with an understanding of the ravages of war.

From 2006 to 2009, the conditions in Iraq deteriorated, and the number of casualties rose steadily. During those years, we heard of new families arriving on a monthly, sometimes weekly basis. Most of the newcomers said the relief agencies had given them a choice of cities. Detroit, renowned for its Arab immigrant population, was full but Cleveland was open. They'd been told the winters were rough, but the price of living was reasonable. And so they came, nuclear families, extended families, and single mothers. Among them were doctors, lawyers, engineers, teachers, and business owners, willing to flounder in a new country so their children could succeed.

Whenever the local Iraqi community got word of new arrivals, we showed up with gifts in hand. In apartments scattered all over Cleveland's west side, we heard harrowing stories brought from Iraq, of friends gone out to buy groceries and losing their lives to roadside bombs, fathers assassinated on their way to work, bodyguards shot at front doorsteps, children kidnapped on their way to school. We heard of suitcases packed haphazardly, a lifetime of belongings abandoned in houses far grander than the four walls these newcomers now called home.

These stories made the Iraq War more real to me than any of the country's past conflicts. I'd come of age learning about the Iran–Iraq War, and the Gulf War and its sanctions, by listening in on adult conversations. My siblings and I were never spoken to directly about Iraq. We were merely admonished to finish our plates with the mention of starving Iraqi children. We were told we'd have nightmares if we snuck peeks at the contraband Arabic newsmagazine circulating among my parents' friends, the one with pictures of brutally wounded child soldiers. Growing up, the only impression I had of Iraq was one of vast blistering suffering. Those of us born in America were the guilty survivors, raised on an excess of food and American television, distant from our culture, the owners of shamefully sparse Arabic vocabularies.

But within this community, I was useful in exile for the first time. I edited the résumés and college applications of

our new arrivals, wrote letters, and made calls. Someone
was benefitting from my English.

Like Khawla, a striking woman in her early forties and
the mother of three boys. She had been a teacher in Baghdad
and the wife of an engineer. Now she was a single mother
living in a Lakewood apartment. Her husband had worked at
a power plant and was suspected to have been killed by insur-
gents with something to gain from keeping the power off.
Prior to this, she'd enjoyed a comfortable life, surrounded by
family and friends, never wanting for money or help with her
children. She never thought one day she'd be living in America without a husband, that she'd have to support her children
alone and learn a new language.

At her secondhand dining table, we studied together.
She tutored me in Arabic and I tutored her in English. She
was sharp, a fast learner who didn't ask me to translate anything for her. She only wanted me to correct the essays she'd
labored through with her "best friend," the nickname she'd
given to her Arabic–English dictionary.

The afternoon her ESL teacher assigned an essay on a
terrible day in your life, Khawla told me of searching for her
husband and winding up in the midst of a car bomb. The
blast picked her up and threw her against a wall. When she
came to, she was certain she was in hell. Bits of blood and
flesh from the exploded bodies had burrowed into her mouth
and nose, and clung to her face and clothes.

"In those days," she added, "people would bring in their
clotheslines and find the same kind of pieces of bodies on
their clothes and sheets."

Now I was the one on the frontlines, bringing home stories to tell my parents. I told them about Khawla, about our

friends who'd just gotten word of cousins who'd left Iraq for London, only to be caught in a roadside bomb on their first visit home. "They said the only way they recognized them was from the pounds in their pocket." Then there was the horrific tale of the Sunni and Shia newlyweds, kidnapped on their honeymoon. Their parents got a phone call, telling them where to pick up their children. When they arrived, all they found were two bodies in garbage bags.

But as Iraq fell apart on sectarian lines, Cleveland's Little Iraq fused closer together. The eating, the visiting, and the gathering continued—a birthday party for a family's first child born in America, a Quran ceremony for the deceased, a tea party to distract someone missing a wedding back home.

My parents and their friends had spoken of the siblings' weddings they'd missed, the funerals they'd only imagined from afar. Now I was watching these emotions play out firsthand—the grief a missed happy occasion could inspire, the regret that could take mourning to excruciating heights, the nagging question of whether the costs of coming to America had been too high. Through the tears, I heard the same line over and over again: "If it was for me, I wouldn't have come, but we have to endure this for our children."

There is no word for "stress" in Arabic with the same con-notation of strain on one's physical and mental well-being, and so many of the newest arrivals say of the American lifestyle "*Kulla* stress," using the English word in an other-wise Arabic sentence. They have adopted the word "busy" as well. "*Ani sayra haweya* busy," they say when they fall behind in their social calls. They say it with regret because there is a loneliness to their new lives they cannot shake.

Cleveland's Little Iraq is becoming a hybrid just like this

mix of Arabic and English, just like me. Every year that
passes, I watch the Iraqi children's accents drop away. They
arrived not knowing more than a handful of words, but now
their tongues have swallowed English, adore English, think
and dream and play in English.

On New Year's Eve, we gather in the apartment of friends.
One of our recent arrivals plays the guitar. I can't sing along
to any of the Arabic songs our group belts out with relish.

In between songs, our hostess asks me, "Are you bored?"

Over the years, my friends have come to know the limits
to my vocabulary; they can anticipate the cultural references
that I will miss. They are sensitive to this, but I no longer
am. This is the gift living in Cleveland has given me. It has
made me comfortable in my role as a translator, a bridge.

"Let's find an English song," she calls out.

Our guitarist strums the tune to "Hotel California." The
lyrics leave our mouths, off-key, sometimes thick and ac-
cented, but familiar to everyone.

Geography of the Heartland

JOHN LLOYD CLAYTON

A Night at the Golden Lion Lounge

I

Gary's really not a bad guy. He always gives some bit of advice or counsel gleaned from years of trial and tribulation. He's a good listener. He smiles and he means it. He always remembers your name. But I'd cover his tab for a month if he would just stop referring to everybody in the place as "old queens" and "us old fags." Invariably this begins complaints about his poor health, his doctor appointments up at Good Sam, his medications, his surgeries, and the daily aches and pains that cause him to be unable to work a normal job. With a face that has lost all decorum and droops like a basset hound's, he drinks gin and tonics by the liter, wears flimsy plastic sandals that show his hairy, bulbous toes, and works from home as a telephone operator for an HMO. Finished with his litany of pains and his sixth G&T, he falls into far-too-detailed reminiscences about his lost loves. When the crowd has turned and every man begins looking down at his watch, he ends by invoking all of us in the drama: "Well, you know, Dorothy just needs a good hard fuck now and then!"

This might turn a few heads at one of the trendy coffee shops down the street. But he's saying it at the Golden Lion

Lounge, the kind of Cincinnati gay bar where time has less stopped than never actually caught up in the first place. You could find it at Clifton and Ludlow, right in the middle of a municipal neighborhood that was swanky a hundred years ago, became a drug-infested slum after the war, then in the nineties became an eclectic neighborhood of French bakeries, Indian restaurants, and clothing shops selling hemp jewelry and organic cotton tees/at 45 bucks a pop. UC is just up the street and DAAP kids pace the sidewalks, intentionally scuffing their $400 sneakers so they look all broken in and worn.

Golden Lion, however, has never changed. It has no windows. It stands upright covered in dull beige plaster from sidewalk to roof. It has no sign, though legend says affixed to the other side of the plywood plank that serves as a door were some sticky letters unevenly applied, the kind you use on your mailbox. But you heard others call it "Golden Lions" and so you did the same. Take away the cellular phones and color photographs and it could be 1929, you sliding in with your brother-in-law after a terrible day on the stock market. Stonewall could be two days away. That eighty-six Camaro parked out back? It might actually just be new. Gary himself might range from thirty to sixty-eight, but in this light he's ageless.

II

I have never been much on bars in general, and a detailed chronicle of my experience with the Cinti gay scene would make little more than a frightened haiku *("Hey Handsome-Lookin?"/ Snarls the sketchy lumberjack/ Time to run back home)*. For actual drinking I prefer, like George Thorogood, to do it alone, and for company I prefer some place with at least a forty-watt light bulb and an off chance that we'd remember the conversation the next day. And I could live out my days just fine without a four-hour loop of Janet Jackson's *Rhythm Nation* set to a dubbed house-mix tape.

I came out of the Bible Belt, where drinking, bars, and gays were things that only occurred in the back pages of pamphlets with titles like "Beware the Devil's Handiwork" or "Don't be Fooled by Satan." My hometown claimed a "diverse religious community" because we had both Presbyterians *and* Baptists. A debate still raged whether or not full-water immersion during the baptismal rite was required for salvation. One sect promised hell for anybody who played musical instruments in church. We were a dry county until 2012, when after 150 years we went "moist" and you could get a glass of cheap table red at a restaurant. It typically stayed open for three days and was stored in the refrigerator. And there were *two* gay guys in town; they'd managed not only to find each other and start a beauty parlor, but also to end with a lover's quarrel that put one of them in jail for assault with a deadly weapon. *Yadda yadda yadda*, Elaine says, and somehow one Tuesday night I found myself on my own stool at the Golden Lion Lounge. I then found myself there again a few times a week for nearly a year.

The first time I walked in, even before my eyes adjusted to the dark, the soundtrack to *Cruising* seemed to echo in my soul and I feared for my life. Sketchy lumberjack? This place was something from *Silence of the Lambs*. But I breathed, sat down, and ordered the finest craft beer on tap . . . Bud Light. As the bartender slid it across to me, I worked frantically on my cover story and a good excuse to run on home: I had narcoleptic children who were being left all alone at home with a box of matches. My baked Alaska needed to set. I was having an aneurysm.

It took me a while to get my sea legs and be able to discern the overall décor. The interior was dark; mahogany veneer on the walls and two fluorescent light bulbs somehow made it darker. The corners were invisible and the ceiling receded away into some sort of netherworld of grime and asbestos tiles. The floors were plastic linoleum that may once have been green, but now were brownish black and covered in mauve, teal, and puce rugs bought more or less new, but on sale as factory seconds in 1974. There was a pool table with threadbare felt, and a bar of black-painted plywood edged in cracked cushioned pleather. It was splitting in most places and covered in duct tape where the foam insulation wasn't already poking out. The metal-framed bar stools matched, and on the far side was a small dance floor with spotty mirrors and a portable sound system purchased along with the rugs and at the same percentage discount. Nobody danced.

There was also a large rear-projection television, one that was very posh in 1983 but that since the mid-nineties had only a ten-inch-square area in the upper right corner still functioning. Over time, like a shrinking universe, it just got smaller and smaller. Later I learned that at some point it stopped working altogether and was positioned out in front of the bar on the sidewalk for months until the fire marshal threatened a violation.

III

I can't say that I was ever a regular, but "semi-regular" just doesn't have the same ring. I never could figure out why I went, and each time I said that trip would be my last. Back at home and scrubbing in the shower with steel wool, I'd lament life and wonder whether an itchy monk's habit and a cloistered cell were in my future. Nights would be lonely, no doubt, but there would be gardening, calligraphy lessons, and barrels of craft beer. Invariably, though, a few days later I'd go back into the Lounge, sit down, and get a decent buzz and three hours' entertainment that, including tip, finished out at about $10.50.

I also learned these things about the bar and about life in general:

Happy hour really neither stopped nor started. Well drinks seemed never to be more or less than $3 and pints of beer were always $2.50, the particular variety rotated by whatever was closest to the expiration date. Well drinks were almost all the same, differing only by color. Good tippers might actually get Coke in a Jack'n'Coke, but sometimes the glass came back just a touch yellower than the Schweppes tonic water.

Each night had a theme: Half-Price Monday, Go-Go Dancer Tuesday, DJ Flash Wednesday, College Night Thursday. Nothing really changed on these nights, though; I heard stories about and saw a picture of DJ Flash, but I never saw him in person. In the picture he was wearing hot pants, cheap shoes, and a three-day beard. College Night Thursday might promise something new, but I don't know that I ever saw anybody under thirty who wasn't being paid to be there or was only there long enough to deliver a crate of booze.

I got to know the regulars pretty well; they were typically the only other people in the place. There was a sixty-something white businessman who called himself Jim and had one whiskey sour before going home to his wife and children. There was a black guy who used to be in the military and rode a motorcycle; he had excellent taste in music, even though the jukebox in the corner didn't work and so we could only hum or talk about our favorite cuts from *Exile on Main Street*. There was a haggard drag queen in a red wig and cotton skirt who never bothered to shave. And of course there was Gary every day after four. Together we solved many of the world's problems, and let the others go without comment. The drag queen tied back her hair and stopped pitching her voice; she had a lovely bass and I bet could sing a mean ballad. Jim complained about his wife; she wanted to renovate the kitchen and he wondered if he could do it without going downtown for the permits. Gary was lonely and never quite asked me on a date, but inched his stool closer and closer, getting within arm's reach by the end of the night. Somebody would buy me a beer. I'd buy somebody a 7-and-7. Nobody ever went home with anybody else, and nobody ever really talked about dates. We were all just there, in the dark and house music, wondering what "Go-Go Dancer Tuesday" was ever meant to be.

IV

The world lost the Golden Lion Lounge in late 2011. Whether it was due to lack of customers, failure to pay taxes, or the zoning board finally realizing the place ought to be condemned, I can't say. I also can't say I was really saddened by the news; I had moved from Cinti and it had been at least a year before that since I'd been back to the bar.

Instead, the image of Cinti that came to mind was

Martha, dozy and pensive on her perch, the last of billions of passenger pigeons that died at the Cinti Zoo in 1914. Nobody much cared about the pigeons when they were alive; they were ubiquitous, harmless, and not particularly good looking. Apparently you could walk right up to a group of them and clobber them all over the head before any one of them would realize something was amiss. But when they were gone, the world suddenly seemed an emptier place. Keep your hawks and falcons and cardinals; I guess people realized that sometimes the world needs a big, ugly bird that never really bothered anybody.

Of course there are and were other gay bars in Cinti. There is a nice, clean, glitzy one across the river where all the college kids and fancy people go; at least one piece of Dolce & Gabbana is required for admission. And if your cologne isn't Gaultier Le Male, it had at least better be one of its seasonal variations. There was also that post-industrial wasteland down by the old train station; new and decorated in steel and concrete and metal. There was a lot of leather there and the phrase "$3 well drink" might as well have been spoken in Farsi; you'd be looking at six bucks for a Coors Light.

Jim and Gary would never go to these places. Neither would I, for that matter. And the drag queen would have to do a lot of waxing beforehand if she tried. Without Golden Lions, I saw us all instead in varying types of lounge chairs, alone in our living rooms, mixing a tumbler and pretending we hadn't actually bought (and were then playing) a solo album by Annie Lennox. When it was there, we never really loved it and just showed up for a few hours; but now, with it gone, we looked around and weighed our other choices.

While those other bars might have nicer décor, more

variation, and better names, they also market the one true thing Golden Lions lacked: attitude. Each has a theme; you have to be somebody to go in there, whether it be a good-looking blonde in a tank top or a daddy vying for first prize in this week's Peter Marino–look-alike contest. And even then they all end up looking the same. Nobody really cared at Golden Lions: if you showed up on a Tuesday in a suit, great. Wednesday, if you came in a flower-checked muumuu, not an eyebrow would be raised. And nobody would send out a team of bloodhounds if you didn't show up on Thursday. It was College Night, after all, and so anticipation of fresh meat would be high.

Instead, it was just nice to have a place that was as un-trendy in 1978 as it was in 2008, a place as dark and dismal on a Monday as it was on a Saturday, and where a pint of flat beer would always, always be $2.50.

RYAN SCHNURR

Family Bones

MY GREAT-GRANDFATHER WAS NEARLY SIXTY years old when he dug a basement in his backyard and built part of a house on top of it. When I say dug a basement I mean he walked out his back door one day with a shovel and started digging. By the time I came around the project was long finished, and there was a garden between the house and the shed that he tended with great care. My great-grandparents lived in that house for fifty-seven years; it is the closest thing my family has to a homeplace.

This place I'm talking about is on East Wilson Street in Oxford, Indiana. Three houses in on the right. The house is white, with a nice big porch on the front and flowers hanging in a pot on the corner. I don't know if the flowers are still there, though. Grandpa's big green desk with the magnifying glass hanging over top is in the spare bedroom to the right, and the kitchen smells like those small, round sausage patties and maple syrup. The upstairs attic is big and hot; Grandpa's journals line the shelves in one corner, and there's a foggy window that looks down through the bathroom vent from up there. Family legend has it that Dan Patch was born pretty much in the backyard. (For a long time I thought Dan Patch was a politician; it turns out he was a record-breaking race-horse at the turn of the twentieth century.) There's an agro plant across the street, or at least there was. Last time I was at the house I didn't even recognize the place: the eaves were falling down on one corner of the porch, and the backyard was a tangled mass of weeds and long grasses.

What's funny is I can tell you how to get there, but even if you follow my directions to the letter we might not end up in the same place.

"Grandpa always took good care of the place," my mom told me last time I mentioned the house to her. It means more to her than it does to me, I think; she lived there some as a kid, and my grandparents loved her. She has a photo of them in front of the side porch of the house. It's bright out, in the picture, and they're squinting pretty heavily. My mom told me that this picture was taken when we went to help them pack up their stuff to move to an assisted-living facility in Fort Wayne, two and half hours northeast of their home.

Ralph and Maxine Swim are actually our great-grandparents, but my siblings and I have always just called them Grandma and Grandpa. Grandpa kept a daily journal for most of his life, written in pencil in your basic college-ruled notebooks. I can remember him sitting in his chair at night, recording the weather patterns and the day's events as well as notes on the books he was reading. For a long time I thought that these had been sold off in the move to Fort Wayne. They've been stored away for most of my adult life. Somewhere. Nobody's sure exactly where. In a storage facility, maybe, or some boxes in the back of a garage—family bones rotting in an unmarked grave.

———

The thing about being ambiguously white in America is that you're simultaneously everything and nothing. Our legacy is forward; we hit the eastern seaboard running and never looked back. It's about mobility. It's about freedom. It's about progress and futures and 401(k)s. Growing up in the suburbs, you don't learn how to look backward to find strength: you don't have to know your history to make it. I don't remember when I first realized this; it just sort of surfaced in the process of trying to find my roots and discovering I didn't recognize the tree. I am not talking about immediate family. I am talking about history. I am talking about knowing where you come from, and the strength of generations.

I am a child of colonizers whose roots, I have long believed, run shallow across the face of the continent. My culture, as a function of its tendency toward domination, is largely invisible. I don't carry on any traditions; I know little of my heritage. The closest thing I have is a childhood steeped in the evangelical church, my dad's small furniture business, and the hole my grandfather dug behind this house in Oxford, Indiana.

I was thirteen years old when my great-grandfather died— old enough to miss him, but not yet old enough to know why.

Ralph Davis Swim, to use the name on his obituary, worked for the United States Postal Service most of his life, minus a short stint in the army, first running the mail trains through St. Louis, Chicago, and Detroit, then at the post office in nearby Lafayette. At his funeral, my grandma (his daughter) told me that he saw the St. Louis Arch go up day by day as he rode the rails in and out of the city. My mom told me she remembers him sitting in his office memorizing the maps of these cities, and that he could pretty well draw them out from memory. Apparently he was the one who would sort the mail by street for drop-off.

I know a few other things about my great-grandfather: I know that he put the same amount of change in his pocket every morning. I know that he labeled everything with small typewritten notes on strips of paper. I know that he was fascinated by engineering—when they started building wind farms in Oxford he would go out and watch them, peppering the builders with questions and suggestions. He is the only person I've ever known who actually used a handkerchief, and he loved to work with his hands, building little sets of drawers and child-size chairs for my brother and sisters and me. (One of these sets of drawers sits in the hallway of my apartment now.) There's a video clip in the family archives of Grandpa raking leaves at my parents' house. He was always raking leaves or doing dishes or something like that at everybody's houses. I am helping him, in the clip, though since I am about four years old I am mainly just spreading the leaves around.

"This will be a history of Ralph and Maxine Swim." *Written by Ralph.*

The document was tucked away in the back of a binder: seven sheets, one-sided, stapled together. It's handwritten in my grandpa's distinctive cursive scrawl; I've seen it a hun-

dred times, on pieces of paper taped inside handmade cub-
bies and inscribed on the inside cover of books. The pages
are photocopies of photocopies of (probably) photocopies.
There's no date, but context clues tell me he wrote it some
time after he retired (1981) and before they moved out of the
house (1998). It is a short document, considering the fact
that it encompasses something like seventy-five years, but
it's obvious that this isn't meant to be comprehensive. It's a
short rundown of facts, names, and dates, with just a bit of
commentary.

Sometime in September, 1939, Ralph [STRIKETHROUGH]
we started working on a farm two miles south of Covington Indi-
ana. A house was furnished to them [STRIKETHROUGH] us
and that was their [STRIKETHROUGH] our first home.

It's written in a mix of third and first person, though he
went through and corrected dozens of pronouns after the fact
in an attempt to create a uniform voice. He glosses over large
sections, and goes into meticulous detail on others—there's a
particularly specific section giving an account of every car
they ever owned—with shorthand names for places like "the
Scott House" and "Old MacDonald's Farm." He recounts
their first few years together, in which they bounced around
from job to job, place to place, struggling to put down roots.
Somewhere in there they had their first daughter, Delores,
whom I know better as Grandma Dee.

The writing is simple, with little embellishment, but its
simplicity brings with it occasional, devastating clarity—
lines that sneak up on you and smack you in the back of the
knees. One such passage is on the third page, around 1943:

It was while we were living in the Scott house that I was
drafted into the army. We considered the fact that I might not

come back from the war. So we shopped for a house so Maxine and Delores would have a home.

I read this section repeatedly, nine or ten times at first, unable to move past it. *We considered the fact that I might not come back from the war.* What a line to write—no, what a line to live. I wonder if he ever realized what grew out of such an experience—the home they purchased was the homeplace I know: 603 East Wilson Street, Oxford, Indiana. Here is when they put down my roots.

I can't prove it, really, but I think my grandparents sort of gave up once they moved to the assisted-living facility. Separated from the community they had lived in for decades, their church, home, and friends, there was a sort of deep and abiding grayness. The move to a nursing home is a symbolic one and my grandpa, especially, didn't like what it was saying; people kept telling him that at eighty-something he was too old to take care of his house anymore, but I don't think he ever believed them. The assisted-living facility was called Golden Years, and I always felt like that was some sort of joke.

This was also about the time that they discovered frozen dinners and packaged snacks. Or rather, the time that they decided that it was okay to start using them. When I was a little kid they took great delight in having us over and gathering the family around the table for home-cooked meals, often with ingredients from their garden. But at Golden Years they would just step into the pint-size kitchen and pop in a toaster pastry or a Stouffer's pot pie. I can't blame them for it, of course. I'm just observing.

A few years after my grandpa died, I started going to high school a mile down the street from Golden Years. After school I would walk over and eat microwavable pot pies with my grandma, and she would tell me stories. Simple ones. Small ones. Ones about my mom; ones about grandpa; ones about the neighbors. Including obscure details yet skipping over huge sections. Like reading Grandpa's family history. On the rare occasion that I can get over myself long enough to consider my blessings, I think a lot about those afternoons.

After I went to college, Grandma moved to a more intensive assisted-living facility. I would travel home to see her, and she would be sitting in her chair by the window, watching the hummingbirds feed. (Grandma always had hummingbird feeders around, and they let her put one outside her window at the new place. I think when she looked out there and let her mind wander she could almost believe she was back in Oxford.) I was there when she died, with my mom and dad and a few other family members.

The peculiar thing about people who are dying of old age is that they stop looking like themselves quite a while before the actual event. It's a different period for everybody—I think my grandpa started about a year before, and my grandma maybe three.

My mom was sitting on the bed when Grandma died. She leaned in and kissed her on the cheek. I heard a faint whisper: "Thank you for loving me." You could tell that Grandma's breaths were getting longer and more laborious, and the world felt like it was slowly getting darker.

"Ryan, I think it's time to go get the nurse."

I walked down the hallway toward the nurse's station. The world was definitely dark now; I could hardly see.

"I think she's gone," I said when I got there. But this was just a formality—I already knew.

My wife, Anna, never met my grandma. But she got really close. I postponed our first date to go to the funeral.

We drove by the homeplace after my grandma died, when we went down to bury her next to my grandpa. It was like going from one graveyard to another. The house was pretty sorry looking; absence filled it like a weight, dragging down the eaves and the corners of its face. My mom would say that you could tell Grandpa hadn't been there in a while, but as I looked out the back window of the car I thought that I saw him moving slowly through the garden, hunched over and wearing his big brown rubber rain boots. And then I saw Grandma standing on the porch, wiping her hands on her apron and waving us in. And this is the funny thing about places: you could show up there and see a dumpy old house across from an agro plant, but I can't help but visit my family.

I don't carry on any traditions. I know little of my heritage. But my family bones fill these holes in the ground in Oxford, Indiana.

JAMES D. GRIFFIOEN

The Fauxtopias of Detroit's Suburbs

DETROIT ROSE TO ITS GREATEST height (and fell as far as it did) in part because Henry Ford didn't want to work too hard. As a child, he hated farm tasks that required physical labor; a neighbor once recalled young Henry as the "laziest little bugger on the face of the earth."[4] Ford's lifelong love of mechanical processes was born out of frustration with manual labor: "I have followed many a weary mile behind a plough and I know all the drudgery of it," he said. "When very young I suspected that much might somehow be done in a better way." Science fiction writer Robert A. Heinlein might have had men like Ford in mind when he said, "Progress isn't made by early risers. It's made by lazy men trying to find easier ways to do something." Ford worked hard to change our very understanding of work. His fanaticism for efficiency led to the Highland Park assembly line; the five dollars his line workers took home each day eventually led them to the middle class; the cars they bought with that money eventually took them to the suburbs.

---

[4] Steven Watts, *The People's Tycoon: Henry Ford and the American Century* (New York: Vintage, 2006), 14.

When he was sixteen, Henry Ford moved from his family's farm in the opposite direction, to downtown Detroit, where he worked as a machinist and later as an engineer for the Edison Illuminating Company. Ford worked so close to his home at 58 Bagley Avenue that he would often sneak off to his own workshop (while still on the clock) to tinker away at the one-cylinder internal combustion engine that would power his quadricycle. When the time came to take it out for a test drive, he discovered that the door to his workshop was too narrow, so he famously knocked down a wall to drive the vehicle out into the streets of the sleepy, horse-drawn metropolis. They say Henry didn't invent the automobile, but that night he might have invented the garage door with his sledgehammer.

A few years later, Detroit was in the midst of its gilded age and was the fourth-largest city in the United States. If you couldn't find work in the auto factories there were jobs building skyscrapers meant to rival those in Chicago and Manhattan, or plenty of other jobs serving the growing population. Historic old Detroit needed to make way for the new. During this time countless historic structures were demolished to make way for new construction. By 1926, Henry Ford's former home and workshop stood in the way of a new theater to be built on the site and was reportedly demolished before construction began. Completed in August, the 4,050-seat Michigan Theater was designed in the French Renaissance style, with a four-story lobby decorated with European oil paintings and sculptures, faux-marble columns, and giant chandeliers. At its unveiling, the Michigan Theater seemed to embody Detroit's decadent optimism for the century ahead, fueled by the surging sales of the automobiles the city and its citizens built. A plaque on the outside of the theater identified it as sitting on the spot where sparks met the tinder of the burgeoning industry.

Meanwhile, in suburban Dearborn, Henry Ford was nearing the end of his decade-long effort overseeing the construction of a sprawling new factory down the Rouge River from his Fairlane estate. The Rouge was Ford's opus, the largest vertically integrated factory in the world, and embodied nearly all of the innovations and ideas he had spent his lifetime developing. Upon its completion in 1928, he walked away from it, retreating to a plot of land just up-river from the factory, where he'd built a painstaking replica of the childhood farm where he'd learned so many early lessons about hard work. The man who'd helped usher in a new, twentieth-century way of living abandoned it to focus his energy on re-creating the nineteenth-century past he'd left behind. He spent much of his time and wealth collecting the artifacts and buildings that would become a different part of his legacy, the major regional tourist attraction known as Greenfield Village and the Henry Ford Museum.

Today 1.5 million people annually visit nearly one hundred historical buildings "preserved" in the walled 240-acre compound, many of them chosen and situated to represent a typical American village between 1870 and 1910. Many of the buildings represent people or places significant to Ford's vision of industrial progress (the Wright Brothers' bicycle shop, Thomas Edison's Menlo Park laboratories), but the heart and soul of Greenfield Village are the buildings associated with Ford's own life and the growth of his automobile company.

Ford deeply regretted not saving his former home and

workshop, which stood in the way of the Michigan Theater, and he was forced to settle for a full-scale replica of the workshop.

But then in 1929, Ford's friend Charles B. King discovered that the original home had not actually been destroyed, but jacked up on rollers, moved, and turned ninety degrees so that it now faced Grand River Avenue; 56–58 Bagley had been given a modern facade at 514 Grand River and was open to the public as the Lola Bett Tea Room. The house where Henry Ford lived when he built his first car was now where the before-theater crowd went for pots of Earl Grey and cucumber sandwiches.

Ford rushed downtown and confirmed it. After negotiating with the owner to buy and remove the house, and replace a large number of its bricks, he ordered his workers to incorporate the bricks into the replica workshop he'd already built at Greenfield Village. According to Ford biographer Sidney Olson, the workers accidentally took bricks from what would have been Number 56 Bagley—the wrong half of the duplex—and to this day at Greenfield Village you can visit the bricks from Henry Ford's neighbor's home that were used to re-create a replica of the workshop where he built his first automobile.

The Lola Bett Tea Room was later demolished to no fanfare. The site, like so much of historic downtown Detroit, is now a parking lot. The lavish theater that originally displaced Henry Ford's workshop met a better-documented fate. By the 1960s, the decadent optimism of its unveiling had faded with its carpets as Detroit faced recompense for its Jazz Age giddiness. The badly neglected Michigan Theater barely survived to show grindhouse double features and host rock con-

certs. In 1976, it closed for good. When it was discovered
that demolition would compromise the structural integrity of
the adjoining office building, the interior of the theater was
gutted to create a 160-space parking garage. Today, commut-
ers park in a three-story garage with gilded seraphim of the
old proscenium arch looking down at them from above the
shredded remnant of a maroon velvet curtain.

It is arguably Detroit's most breathtaking ruin, beloved by
photographers, journalists, and academics for the easy irony
of Ford automobiles parking in a ruined theater on the site
of the garage where Henry Ford built his first automobile.
What's more interesting, I think, is how this building represents a sort of unintentional preservation. At least this is not
just another surface lot. And with so much of the rest of the
historical city lost to development, demolition, and abandonment, there is the deeper irony that fifteen miles away Henry
Ford moved so many historical buildings brick by brick from
elsewhere around the country and "preserved" them as de-
contextualized structures in a counterfeit community.

The nostalgic fantasy of small-town life on display at Greenfield Village is what most of the beneficiaries of Ford's
$5-a-day plan thought they would get when they left Detroit
for the small towns surrounding it: they sought a pastoral
atmosphere, far from the clanging of streetcars, factories, and
crime. "We shall solve the city problem by leaving the city,"
Ford said. With his cheap automobiles, anyone with the
salaries he provided could escape the dirty city's ethnic
neighborhoods, and (like Philip Roth's Swede Levov in
American Pastoral) cast away their immigrant shadows. With

the fresh air and personal fiefdoms found on every new block of the suburbs, anyone could be baptized as an American in that most American of places: the small town. Frozen in time, Greenfield Village serves as the perfect template for this utopia. Aside from the occasional sputtering of ubiquitous Model Ts (the only cars permitted inside Greenfield Village's walls), the roads are safe for foot traffic. There is no graffiti or crime of any kind. There are plenty of options to buy old-fashioned crafts or dine on historical comfort food. Everything is wholesome and good. And none of it is real.

Like some medieval village, Greenfield Village is surrounded by a ten-foot wall. You must drive there and leave your car in a vast surface parking lot before paying $24 to get inside (parking is an additional $5).

Every night the streets are emptied and the gates locked and guarded. Even the costumed interpreters abandon the village for four months every winter. Henry Ford, the man who famously said, "History is bunk," spent the last part of his life building an unoccupied historic village without any actual history. It has now existed there for eighty years. New buildings and attractions have been added, but since it was created in the 1930s it remains perpetually and intentionally frozen in the 1890s. This village Henry Ford built has, for eighty years, existed solely as a simulacrum of the world Henry Ford destroyed.

If Greenfield Village represents the sort of wholesome, idyllic (and sanitized) environment that most Detroiters sought in the suburbs, then the city of Detroit has for several decades come to represent its opposite: seedy, gritty, blighted, ruined, overgrown, dangerous, poor, and black. Yet in the era of exurban sprawl, some parts of Detroit have lost so much housing stock they are starting to resemble the pastoral environment Antoine de La Mothe Cadillac found there two centuries before the city became a symbol of American industrial might (three hundred years before it came to symbolize its failure). Today these parts of Detroit look more like the actual world Greenfield Village has always tried to represent than many of its once-bucolic suburbs.

That's because for the last fifty years, Detroit's suburbs have been where the action is. One of the reasons metro Detroiters get so upset when journalists and photographers represent Detroit as a city of ruins is the reality that there are millions of people living in safe, well-kept neighborhoods in dozens of prosperous suburban communities. Many Detroit suburbs have walkable, thriving business districts that resemble gentrified neighborhoods in other cities. Southfield has more workers and office space than downtown Detroit. But with big-city amenities come big-city issues of traffic, parking, and overcrowding. And of course, most suburban open spaces long ago gave way to subdivisions, strip malls, and parking lots for shopping malls and big-box stores.

With all the recent development and growth, it is easy to forget that these suburbs of Detroit have their own histories. There was a time before sprawl when these small, historic communities and their citizens provided the lumber for Detroit's homes and the food for its tables. Last year, I started taking an interest in the histories of these communities and visiting all the historical museums and sites that I could find. There are dozens of historical societies in these suburban Detroit communities, many of them quite active. I quickly learned that in more than eighteen suburban communities, an effort had been made since the 1970s to preserve historical structures that were "in the way of development" through the creation of a series of historic "towns" (basically mini–Greenfield Villages) that surround Detroit in every direction the highways go.

Over the past few months, I've visited each of these historic parks to observe and document what so many communities surrounding Detroit did when their history was threatened by sprawl—after all, the drastic and sudden change that sprawl brings to a small town is as devastating to its history and overall character as upper- and middle-class flight was to the city of Detroit. By the 1970s, the suburban pioneers who first moved to these communities were getting older, and it was clear that the small-town atmosphere they sought there was doomed. The newer residents of the new subdivisions were just another kind of immigrant seeking refuge and hope in a new place. And there were millions of them. I was interested in the idea of history each suburban community has preserved and presented in villages where no one would actually work or live and where none of the buildings had been preserved in their original context. What did they want their history to look like? Where would they fit that history now that land had grown so scarce? I photographed each village in the state in which they spent most of their time: vacant, empty, and silent (some even behind locked gates).

These communities all preserved and presented a nearly identical set of nineteenth-century buildings to create eerily similar, lifeless fauxtopias. Each boasts at least one pioneer log cabin, a rescued one-room schoolhouse, a small church, and a general store.

These are the structures that form the bedrock of community: the rustic hearth, with separate spaces for education, religion, and commerce. These historic parks are perfect symbols of the romantic small-town fantasy most people first thought they would get when they moved out of the city. That today they are besieged on all sides by freeways clogged with rush-hour traffic, thriving businesses and office parks, and neighborhoods full of homes shows that no one escaped the city: they brought the city with them.

I keep thinking about those bricks Henry Ford knocked out of a perfectly functional building and hauled back to his walled town to incorporate into a replica of a modest turn-of-the-century workshop. What did he think those bricks meant? What strange power did he believe they held? Does it even matter, in the end, that the bricks came from the wrong house, when the underlying idea of moving any bricks from one place to another to represent some physical space of historical significance is so ludicrous? What story does a building tell when it has been removed from its original context: the mill from its stream, the general store from the community it served, the log cabin from the path of civilization in which it stood? What does Robert Frost's home in Greenfield Village mean if we can't walk down the same sidewalks he did when we leave it, or past the same hills where he gazed while dreaming up verse? And what about historical buildings rebuilt entirely after they were razed in war or some other disaster? Or historic buildings gutted to shells and filled with Chinese drywall and modern ornament? In the end, is any building really anything more than just mud and carbon?

It seems we are capable of interacting with history only through limited means. The first way is through the tangible. When we hold an antique or view something in a museum, we understand that we are interacting with the same object in the same way as others throughout history. Henry Ford believed very strongly in this tangible history. He created a legacy where future Americans would understand living history through interaction with ordinary objects—that's why he collected so many thousands of ordinary tools and handicrafts and machines. But the second (and perhaps more important) way we interact with history is through the intangible; through our imaginations and the inspiration of others' memories, their spoken or written words or artistic and photographic records. "History is about places of the mind," writes historian David Starkey[5]. Appreciating history through architecture requires some of this imagination. When we visit the Roman Forum, we like to tell ourselves that we are "walking in the footsteps of Caesar," but those bricks and columns have been toppled and rebuilt and broken again before being screwed together by dozens of archaeologists thousands of years after the Republic fell. Still. We believe architecture brings us closer to history the way medieval pilgrims believed relics brought them closer to Christ. They must have known that chunk of wood probably didn't come from the true cross, but still, they bought it. We know a building is really just wood and bricks, but still we tell ourselves it's something more, and open our imaginations to the wonder of those who came before us.

---

[5] https://www.theguardian.com/lifeandstyle/2009/mar/29/david-starkey-historian

I have never lived anywhere so burdened by nostalgia, which is a sort of enemy to history. How many older suburbanites cluck on and on about the state of Detroit today and then wax nostalgic for how good it was in the good old days? If it was so good, why did any of them leave? Most of the folks who live in the communities I've discussed above do not trace their origins to whitewashed steeples or quaint one-room schoolhouses that have been saved as a nostalgic reminder of a past most never really experienced. They trace their stories through Detroit, and the old world beyond it. While Detroit rots, the nostalgic, fauxtopian villages that surround that city are a vision of history some would rather embrace. This is what happens when we try too hard to preserve the past. We create towns without memories. We abandon buildings by saving them. We create history without any history. A history of nowhere. A history that is, I suppose, easier to contend with.

ERIC ANDERSON

Pretty Things to Hang on the Wall

I WANT TO LAUGH WHEN I hear that people are moving to
Cleveland to practice their art. Then I want to spit in their
faces. I want to do them grievous bodily harm. How dare
they, I think. The nerve. Cleveland has never been the kind
of place where it's easy to be an artist; in fact, people who
want to unravel the greater mysteries or search for universal
beauty or answer the unanswerable questions usually leave
Ohio, while those who stay often find themselves using art
as a way to make life on the North Shore more bearable. In
Cleveland, there just aren't that many careers in the arts to
be had. When I told my father I was thinking about going
to the Cleveland Institute of Art, he said, "What kind of
work can you find doing that?"

In fairness, he knew I lacked any sense of practicality. I
wasn't thinking about a career in graphic design. I wanted
something like Warhol, but you know . . . more manly. But
I was young and I didn't have an answer to his question, so
I did what he did. I found a job working construction in the
steel mills.

When my artist friends talk about the dangerous toxic-
ity of things like cadmium red and sprayable fixative, I nod

politely but inside I'm cracking up. During my time as a surveyor in the mills, traveling back and forth between what was then U.S. Steel in Lorain and LTV in Cleveland, I used to see water so polluted that nothing would float in it. I would see dead rats with tumors exploding out of their sides. The old-timers would tell me how much dirtier the mill used to be, before the hippies, before the EPA. The cars in the parking lot would be covered in red dust. Open your lunch box, red dust on the food. Spit, red dust. Cough, red dust. After a rain, the gutters were streaked with something that looked like dried blood.

When I was a boy, my father would come home from the mill and wash his face and hands in the sink; I would tell him about my small day and watch the water turn brown as it swirled. When he was done he would wipe his face on the towel and leave behind the imprint of a red skull; he couldn't wash enough to get clean.

I had a romantic notion that such filthiness was what it meant to be a man. But after a few weeks in the mill, I started dreaming about cancer. There was a story about some geese that landed in the vivid green wastewater–retention basin and sank right to the bottom. I'd imagine my body after death, completely decayed, only a man-shaped pile of rust in my coffin.

Those dreams weren't enough to stop me from going to work, though. From my late teens—in those days when we weren't all pretending a college education matters—until my mid-thirties when I decided that a master's degree in fiction and poetry would somehow make my life better, I kept willingly walking into mills and factories and industrial complexes. Usually these excursions would begin with a brief safety video describing all the ways one was likely to be killed inside. The names on the mills changed: U.S. Steel became USS-Kobe, and LTV, which the old-timers used to call "Good old Liquidate, Terminate, and Vacate," closed and opened and morphed around before becoming Arcelor-Mittal. Each time the names changed, fewer people had jobs.

The name that has stayed with me the most came from LTV: the continuous annealing line. Annealing is a process by which steel is heated and then slowly cooled so that the metal will be tough. Imagine being annealed continuously.

In those spare moments when I wasn't sweating a mortgage payment or trying to coax some education for my children out of the region's essentially rotten school system, I pretended to be an artist. In school, I was only interested in art and English, and after graduation I clung to those two things as a justification for why I was wasting my life working construction all over northeast Ohio. I fancied myself as one of those artists who would speak for common people, never really imagining myself as one of the commoners. The most consistent thing in my life was the terrible impracticality of my art. I wrote novels and sent poems to *The New Yorker*. On job sites, I would collect materials and wire them into sculptures—it's hard to be discreet when you're wiring rebar and scraps from the carpenter's forms into things that look a little bit like birds. Draw a little on the back of a pay stub, paint with a set of cheap watercolors from Pat Catan's. If anyone asked, I would curse my art by calling it a hobby. To be a native-born artist in Cleveland, you must master the art of self-deprecation. You must not let the normal folks know that you have been thinking, now and then, about immortality.

Of course, the newcomers mean well. They have come from other places in the country where it's too hard to be an artist; perhaps the grant money ran out, or the colleges are only hiring adjuncts. It could be that the inspiration just disappeared, as inspiration sometimes does.

Since it's so hard to be paid to live as an artist in Cleveland, the aspirant lives somewhere cheap. This neighborhood usually features a housing project and some boarded-up factories. Someone calls an abandoned warehouse a loft. A few more artists show up, and someone opens a gallery. Soon there's a coffee shop and a diner and a Laundromat. Other people who have artistic temperaments arrive; a few of them mean well, but most of them call themselves artists despite the lack of any real talent. They want to be artists the same way that sports fans want to play shortstop for the Yankees. Instead of skill, they have disposable income. They have investments and trust funds. The coffee shop becomes a Starbucks, the diner an Applebee's. The prices in the galleries reflect what everyone's calling the "growing importance of the movement."

The first sign of the coming apocalypse is the art walk: the Typhoid Marys of gentrification. Developers show up, displaying all the sensitive charm of a multinational corporation. The first thing they fix is the parking situation. They refurbish the factories because that's the kind of news that looks good in the arts section, and they evict the last surviving members of the original neighborhood, the old immigrants and housing project leftovers, because that's the kind of story that appears in a blurb at the back of the city section. Rent goes up. The air is thick with the smell of money. Money smells like being neighbors with a bread factory. Sure, you want to believe that's what heaven smells like. But really, breathing has become a long struggle against yeasty suffocation. Meanwhile, the artists can no longer afford to stay in the neighborhood, and nobody knows what happened to the people who lived there before—shadows remain, or a few splotches of paint in the background of somebody's landscape.

But it's all okay. There's a lot of good space farther out on the West Side or the East Side, cheap rent, a Salvation Army. Everyone's moving there.

It was never really about art. The artists wanted whatever it is that artists want (recognition, a solo show, a mention in a textbook, a cash award, a residency, a sabbatical, to be called a genius by people that other people call geniuses, anything but a job), and the gallery owners made a little money—which they used to pay back their loans, which means the banks made some money, and some developers got rich. People looking for ways to be young and hip and successful mortgaged ridiculously expensive townhouses and brownstones and bought pretty things to hang on the wall. Hanging things on the wall meant decorating the room. Contractors were hired, supplies were ordered, and workmen were paid. How it all trickles down so beautifully! I try my best to believe that, even if only by accident, some human looked at something made by another human and wondered what it all meant.

It's all understandable, and it's shitty, but I can get over that. What I can't and won't get over is how the artists swaggered into town like major leaguers going down to the minors on a rehab assignment. While I spent my time being afraid to want something beautiful, they actually went to art school. Some of them arrived here with a certain kind of fame. Some of them didn't become famous until they saw what we've done to ourselves. Along the way, they dragged a few natives into the brief, burning spotlight. I try not to be jealous. But it's too easy to hate the truly talented. Or the truly connected. Or the lucky.

It's hard not to feel like the details of my working life became their art. *All that beautiful decay,* they seemed to say. *Look at how wonderful this place used to be. Look at how terrible it all was. This region really says something about the world. This says something about our nation. I feel like I've lived here all my life!*

I feel guilty for overstating the problem. Then I feel like I am not overstating the problem at all. They came and looked at my secret fears and told me how interesting they are, and how relevant, and how all that misery makes such a fascinating mosaic, if only I could step back and see how all the details have been arranged.

Yet none of them asked where the rust came from.

There's no way of knowing in the end what matters more: the lives that those mills and factories supported or the art that only exists because those lives no longer exist. In the end, it's not the fact that I or my friends and family feel exploited. It's not that the visiting artists were wrong or even that they were right. What most bothers me is that I wasn't smart enough to exploit the situation for myself. The whole thing was happening all around me, and I was too busy watching what I imagined as real artists watch and document what I called home. All those moments of folly when I gave up my ambitions to pay the bills. All those things that flashed briefly beautiful before I pushed them aside. It all turned out to be art after all. I just missed it.

CAROLYNE WHELAN

King Coal and the West Virginia Mine Wars Museum

WILMA STEELE SITS ON HER screened porch and watches the last of the apples fall from her tree. It's a beautiful, crisp day in Mingo County, West Virginia. Inside, there is still a faint dampness from when the house flooded as the result of nearby mountaintop removal, but on the porch, the dry air has that warm autumn smell of leaves and soil. Steele has lived in this region all her life, and her lineage traces back deep into the earth of Mingo County as far as she can follow it, like light in the abandoned mine shaft down the street. She is one of the founders of the West Virginia Mine Wars Museum[6], located in Matewan, Mingo County, and on October 1, as she accepted a Coal Heritage Award from the Coal Heritage Highway Authority on behalf of the museum, Don Blankenship wrapped up the first day of his closed trial.

Don Blankenship was also born and raised in Mingo County—his mother was a McCoy, a descendant of the infamous enemies of the Hatfields. He and Steele went to school together, but after that, their paths diverged: while

---

6 http://www.wvminewars.com/

Steele became a high school art teacher—and a member of her teachers' union—Blankenship climbed the ladder of corporate coal, ultimately becoming the chairman and CEO of Massey Energy Company and, according to *The New York Times*, "one of West Virginia's most feared and powerful figures[7]," the kind of man who pumps toxic slurry back into the ground to save his company money[8] and throws his breakfast if it's not to his liking[9]. In April 2010, twenty-nine miners died as the result of an explosion at one of Massey's mines, Upper Big Branch; Blankenship subsequently was accused of scheming with others at the company to violate safety rules and deceive regulators. The trial holding a CEO responsible for the deaths of his company's workers was the first of its kind, and the results could set a precedent for future corporate leaders.[10] Although the West Virginia Mine Wars Museum focuses on the history of the region, Steele believes that in light of the Upper Big Branch explosion and the trial, the historical narrative is applicable today.

"The mines used to own people by owning their homes, their stores, their churches, their schools," Steele says. "Now, they don't need to, because they own people's minds. It's much more psychological." The coal companies donate money to the local schools, she says, so the teachers will

---

[7] http://www.nytimes.com/2015/06/21/business/energy-environment/the-people-v-the-coal-baron.html

[8] http://www.rollingstone.com/politics/news/the-dark-lord-of-coal-country-20101129?page=6

[9] http://www.nytimes.com/2015/06/21/business/energy-environment/the-people-v-the-coal-baron.html

[10] Blankenship was found guilty in 2015 of conspiring to violate federal mine safety standards and in 2016 was sentenced to a year in prison, and assessed a $250,000 fine.

endorse the industry. In response to reports of coal-based pollution and sick children, it was the teachers who wrote to the paper to discredit the accusations as liberal propaganda, Steele says, and it wasn't until a reporter visited Marsh Fork Elementary School and with his finger wiped up a layer of coal dirt to show to the camera[11] that the area finally started to take notice.

It wasn't always this way. The region has a rich history of people banding together and pushing back against the industry, dating back to the West Virginia Mine Wars. The wars, which took place from 1910 to 1922—starting with the union aggregation that led to the first official strike in 1912—involved more than ten thousand miners who went on strike repeatedly over low wages and deadly working conditions. The West Virginia Mine Wars Museum chronicles it all, from the Paint Creek–Cabin Creek strike of 1912 to 1913 (one of the worst conflicts in American labor history, with deaths from both malnourishment and hired guards) to the 1920 Battle of Matewan (also known as the Matewan Massacre), in which miners surrounded and killed seven detectives from the Baldwin–Felts Detective Agency who had been hired by mine officials to issue eviction letters. The exhibits culminate with information on the 1921 Miners' March that led to the Battle of Blair Mountain: with ten thousand miners on strike, this was the largest armed uprising of U.S. citizens outside of wartime, and federal troops were called in to break it up. Also included in the museum's collection are artifacts from coal camp life, including a replica of the tent colonies where miner families

---

[11] http://bloodonthemountain.com/

lived when they were kicked out of their company homes for striking. The display curves around in a horseshoe of narrative, starting and ending at the front of the museum, reflective (intended or not) of the cyclical nature of labor movements in general, and of the current chapter unfolding under the omnipresent "King Coal." If the museum narrative were to continue into the present day, Don Blankenship might have his photo in the museum in association with his own wars against laborers: In 1984, a strike at Blackberry Creek against Massey turned bloody and lasted more than a year. Blankenship, for his part, was largely concerned about his television, which, famously, was allegedly shot by pro-union forces.

The first displays upon entering the museum are bookshelves full of historic artifacts, presented without the austerity of glass cases, which keep a barrier between article and viewer. During a tour, Steele takes great care to explain the personal history of an oil lantern used to light the way for the miners. "My dad, he worked in the mine with all different people, and it didn't matter where you were from and what you looked like—if you were union brothers, you were union brothers," she says. "A couple years ago, he went to visit with an old friend from the mine, an African American man, and the friend showed him this old lantern. My dad told him his daughter collected old stuff like this to help preserve it, and the man said, 'Then you give this to your daughter to look after and keep safe.' So it's here now, and to me its presence here in the museum is a tribute not only to my father and to that man, but to the friendship between them, that saw each other as brothers. Funny, isn't it," she muses as she puts the lantern back down, "this article that was created for safety was really just another thing that could have blown up in their faces."

There is a lot of love in the museum that has gone toward making that part of history clear: the role all people had in the labor strikes and mine wars. A picture of a white woman and an African American woman sitting in the kitchen of a factory house is on proud display, and indeed, many of the group photos of union members and of families—including the ones that show people peeping out of the holes slit in tents by the Baldwin–Felts agents hired to destroy the shelters—show people of all backgrounds.

The building where the West Virginia Mine Wars Museum is located was rented for a year and a half prior to the museum's opening. As in much of Matewan, the building is one of the original structures of the town, and still contains bullet holes from the shoot-out between Sid Hatfield, a union sympathizer and the police chief of Matewan during the Battle of Matewan, and the mine's hired guards. Most of the museum's founders had been working together on the project for two years, with creative director and exhibition designer Shaun Slifer joining the team when the space was rented about six months later. Slifer has been installing exhibits for a decade in museums, including the Carnegie Museum of Art, the Frick Art & Historical Center, and others; he also has worked on projects from a people's history perspective in the past, including Pittsburgh's Howling Mob Society signs, which were featured in the 2012 Venice Biennale of Architecture. Additionally, he presented on the National Conference for Historic Preservation, and co-edited the Justseeds Artists' Cooperative's *Firebrands: Portraits from the Americas*, published by Microcosm.

"It is a bit strange to think about a museum coming together so quickly, especially when in Pittsburgh the museums are these official and long-standing establishments," Slifer says. "But there was a lot of work behind the scenes before we got to the place we are now." While the West Virginia Mine Wars Museum may have opened its doors relatively quickly, the same techniques and attention to detail went into the design of this small storefront museum as in those larger-budget spaces. Everything is archival and, once a visitor has entered into the horseshoe past the initial open shelves, the displays all have Plexiglas cases. There are videos of historic newsreels as well as oral histories playing from a parabolic speaker. There is also much to read at each display, and large quotes in vinyl dance along the walls to help guide the narrative.

Prior to the creation of the West Virginia Mine Wars Museum, co-founders Kenny King and Wilma Steele had been a part of the modest Blair Mountain Museum, which has since closed. Both have impressive personal collections of artifacts collected over the years, often handed down from their parents and grandparents, and these treasures, among many others, can be seen now at the tiny museum. King, in fact, may have the world's largest collection of such artifacts, many of which are quite rare; in addition to familial treasures, he actively hunts down items of this era using a metal detector. Among his collection at the museum are bullet casings and clips from a number of guns, including .45 ACP shells for a Thompson submachine gun (also known as a Tommy gun), which would have been brand-new at the time and owned by law enforcement; he also has scrip that reads, "Good for one loaf of bread," which is paired in the museum display with a rare milk bottle (fresh milk would have been inaccessible to most mine workers).

While there is something about the artifacts that feels profoundly American, many items sing of the rich cultural heritage brought overseas by immigrants seeking a better life and finding themselves in the hollow of Matewan. One display at the museum specifically showcases such multicultural relics, though the nods to the miners' homelands can be seen in so many of the photos: kilts and embroidered vests with paisley designs, the clothing of people holding on to their past while working to create a brighter future. That these cultures persevered is ironically the work of the mine owners themselves, who, according to historians of the museum, purposefully kept each culture apart. As immigrants came off the boats in New York, they were offered jobs at the mine, given places to live in their own area of Matewan, and assigned to a shift where they worked according to ethnicity of origin. Cultures were not shared and other languages were not learned, all of which was a tool of the mine owners to avoid unionization—when the miners didn't know each other, they could resent each other and animosity could grow, which kept them from finding common ground for demanding fair wages and safe conditions.

Ultimately, the groups did meet, talk, and unionize. The red bandannas they wore, originally produced in Scotland with designs taken from Hungarian and Persian traditional patterns, are a tribute to that blending. They were worn like a uniform, a simple way to tell who was on their side. One origin of the word "redneck" derives from these bandannas: the term, which is now used with some amount of xenophobia to refer to small-minded people who typically live in rural Southern areas, in this sense is actually a nod to diversity and working together for a common good. In a photo of the burial of Sid Hatfield, funeral attendees can be seen wearing patterns found in the bandannas, as well as Scottish kilts, lace, and other formal attire brought along during long boat rides to America.

"Today," Steele sighs, her gaze extending into the rich green forest just beyond her porch, "without the unions bringing people together, there is more bigotry. Just how they've always wanted it, keeping workers apart instead of fighting together." Steele's husband, Terry, a retired mine worker and member of the United Mine Workers Association (UMWA) union, agrees. The way he sees it, today's workers are paid good wages and when they are let go, it's blamed on the increasing government regulations that cost King Coal money in upkeep. But the regulations are necessary for the people to live, because they affect their own drinking water and air quality, their own children's welfare.

Unions are a contentious topic in Mingo County, with no active miners among the 850 members of the UMWA; many miners blame the union and the government for the hard times miners are facing as interest in coal diminishes. From the union perspective, the main reason people are losing their jobs is because the mine owners—including Blankenship—didn't want to lose money by keeping up with regulations when they could afford it. Meanwhile, some people hate the unions because the unions are getting paid through tax dollars. "But that's only because the mine company didn't pay into the pensions when they had the money and now that they aren't doing as well, they certainly don't want to pay," Terry says.

Indeed, some in King Coal country are doing worse than others. Although Blankenship now lives in Tennessee, he maintained his home in Mingo County until retirement (though once his actions at Massey polluted the water, he did have special plumbing installed to source clean water from outside the county[12]—a luxury not available to his workers and neighbors). Since the Upper Big Branch disaster, critics of Blankenship seem to have no difficulty seeing evil in his beady eyes and villainous mustache. Certainly, they've been given little reason to see anything else. Maybe it's her art-teacher openheartedness, or her love for her fellow West Virginians, but Steele is the first to comment on the complexity of Blankenship: He's not quite evil, and that's perhaps even more dangerous.

"He's the kind of person who really listens to people, really tries to figure out who they are," she says. "When we were in school, he was a nice guy, I mean a really nice person. Everyone liked him. And if somebody didn't, well, they were the jerk, and that was generally known." When asked what happened to make Blankenship grow up to be the type of person who would care so little for his fellows, she could only shrug: "Coal got him." When he originally came to Massey as an office manager, she says, he could have cleaned up a lot of King Coal's practices. Instead, he became known as the leading force against the UMWA.

---

[12] http://www.rollingstone.com/politics/news/the-dark-lord-of-coal
-country-20101129?page=6

When the victims from the Upper Big Branch explosion were autopsied, it was revealed that 71 percent of them suffered from black lung, the deadly coal dust disease. The industry average is 3.2 percent.

Blankenship has visited the West Virginia Mine Wars Museum, presumably curious as to what version of history the museum might tell, and how far back and forward along Mingo County's coal lineage it dared tread. Elijah Hooker, now a board member who was stationed at the museum's front desk during two of Blankenship visits and who spoke with him at length, dismisses any notion of malicious intent. "The mere fact that a young man was working for a museum that is essentially the antithesis to everything in which Blankenship's creed, or system of beliefs, has stood in opposition towards, most likely left him in a state of curiosity," says Hooker via email, in explanation of what interest Blankenship may have had in talking with him. "[He] came to the museum out of genuine motives. After all, Matewan is his home; this museum does impart the history of [his community]. While it may take a particular stance, nevertheless, our attempt is to reconstruct the history of an area deemed to be a forgotten land of no significance to the greater development of America's past; thus, I feel that there was genuine intrigue involved with Don's visit to our museum, one in which no ulterior motives were attached—simply curiosity as to what was going on in the area he considers to be home." Hooker, on his part, does not believe Blankenship is necessarily the monster he's portrayed to be, one who had specific intentions of killing twenty-nine workers, but rather is someone who made some gross errors in judgment during his time as CEO. Perhaps he just saw the dollars and cents of business much more clearly than the people who were hidden in the mines, the ones who put that money in the Massey account.

Still, the tension between King Coal and those preserving its true history is palpable. "He went through the museum and spent over an hour there [during one visit], and it's a very small place. He took pictures, read all the texts," says Dr. Chuck Keeney, museum board member and history professor at Southern West Virginia Community and Technical College. "Then after, he and I spoke for a bit. He and I of course have a different heritage, his background being a union-buster, and I have union leaders in my heritage. So we're on opposite sides." This opposition is a point of conflict for the museum, daring to tell the history of unions in an area whose union members currently are largely retired miners.

"The conflict over coal has become over the years to be a conflict of memory. King Coal is not going to disappear. It's still a powerful force, and a powerful social force," Keeney says, and in this memory and storytelling lies the burden and joy of opening up an independent museum. "We were able to include quotes and facts that a state-sponsored museum wouldn't be able to do. It's quite enjoyable, to not have to be politically correct, to not have to pander to donors who have their own agendas or are concerned about image."

Ultimately, the West Virginia Mine Wars Museum tells the story of a time when coal was everything, and of a future when it might not be. That's certainly the case for Blankenship. Sid Hatfield probably never dreamed of the day when something like a mine explosion would put the company boss on trial, and maybe there is a future for citizens of West Virginia in which mine explosions themselves are an archaic story relegated to Plexiglas displays. In the meantime, we can study our past, celebrate it, and learn from it.

MARTHA BAYNE

Seed or Weed?
ON THE EVOLUTION OF CHICAGO'S BLOOMINGDALE TRAIL

DOWN THE STREET FROM MY apartment there's a community garden on a vacant lot owned by my landlord—although, of course, it's not actually "vacant" at all. It's home to a dozen raised beds of flowers and vegetables. There are hoses and a rain barrel and two rotating compost bins and a mess of stakes and tomato cages under the porch of the house next door. In the spring, mushrooms push up through the dandelions and Queen Anne's lace along the fence.

In the first warm weeks of May I sowed buttercrunch lettuce and mesclun and red romaine, along with beets and chard and kale and carrots in the plots I'd claimed as my own. I had the best intentions. I had carefully ordered an array of exotics from the heirloom seed catalog—Chantenay red cored carrots; bull's blood and golden beets. I amended the soil with compost and an extravagant layer of topsoil. I even drew a map in a little spiral notebook. But, perhaps dizzy with the sudden onset of spring, when I got down in the dirt itself I quickly abandoned any attempt to impose structure on nature and began sprinkling seeds with abandon. I figured I'd thin them out once they'd germinated, after I saw what stuck.

One month later the lettuces were coming up thick in nice straight rows. But the bok choy and the chard looked sketchy, their sprouts emerging from the soil in curves and clumps, if at all. Only four of dozens of beet seeds had germinated, and cilantro had invaded the carrot patch. Samaras from the maple towering to the east rained down on the garden, blanketing it with little brown propellers, and every morning this summer I crouched over the beds, contemplating new clusters of inch-high shoots, wondering, Are you kale or crabgrass? Are you seed or are you weed?

I live half a block north of this garden, on Humboldt Boulevard in Chicago, practically on top of the Bloomingdale Trail. That's the colloquial name given to the elevated tracks stretching 2.7 miles west across the city from Ashland all the way to Ridgeway, along Bloomingdale Avenue, about midway between Armitage and North. Once it was a spur line for the Canadian Pacific Railway, but regular transit stopped on the line in 2001, and in the years that followed the tracks were reclaimed by fast-growing plants. Bull thistles and pokeweed grew thick along the railings while pineapple weed choked the tracks—as did broken glass, beer cans, dead rats, abandoned shoes, needles, condoms, and yards upon yards of VHS tape, scenes from *Ghostbusters* unspooling on the breeze. Catalpa and gingko stretched their branches overhead. Wildflowers rioted in July.

From the ground the trail didn't look like much—a few miles of dank, crumbling cement held together by graffiti. But from above it was a magic highway. A thin strip of rough, scrubby green easily accessed at strategic points along a poorly maintained fence line, the Bloomingdale Trail gave sanctuary to drinkers, dog walkers, joggers, junkies, and anyone seeking shelter from the streets below. It was an interstitial wilderness, opportunistic plants holding tight to rocky soil, and for much of this century's first decade, it was Chicago's best-kept open secret.

These days the weeds are gone. In August 2013 the city broke ground on construction of a long-planned network of parks and trails along the railway that's now called the 606—after the three numbers all Chicago zip codes share in common. Said name change—enacted after much focus-grouping and brand consultation by the consortium of agencies charged with developing the park—seems to have succeeded in offending few, and pleasing fewer, but on the street it doesn't matter. Everyone still calls it the Bloomingdale Trail anyway.

No matter what you call it, it's set to open in its first phase in 2015, after more than ten years of grassroots organizing and prep. Now that the city's taken charge the project is moving full steam ahead. BUILDING A NEW CHICAGO, declare the signs dangling from its bridges, and I've watched over the last nine months as small trucks and front-end loaders zip back and forth along the viaduct past my second-story windows. On the ground, the bright murals that marked the passage from Humboldt Park to Logan Square—whose neighborhood boundary the trail passively polices—have been sandblasted away in the name of lead abatement. The quiet man who lived underneath the overpass all last summer has moved on. If you trespass on the tracks these days you'll get a ticket.

In 1995 I was homeless in Chicago, sleeping on the floor of a friend's loft at Grand and Wood. I spent hours each day, those first weeks, adrift in a strange town, drinking coffee at the old Wishbone on Grand and poring over the *Reader* classifieds looking for a job, an apartment, a map, a clue.

In the afternoons I walked the streets of greater Wicker Park—Grand to North; Ashland to Western—building a muscle memory of Chicago's geography with every step. I didn't go west of Western on my own back then. Back then, to a newbie, west of Western was the wild unknown, best approached only with a trusted guide.

One night we threw a party. My friends were moving out of the loft, moving on, and I needed to as well. We posted a sign in the kitchen, bold black Sharpie on butcher paper: MARTHA NEEDS A PLACE TO LIVE. It was a party with intention, at which I had to introduce myself to strangers over and over until one of them stuck. I moved into Carla's apartment at Augusta and Damen, the perfect center of my daily wanderings, two weeks later. Was the seed of my life in Chicago planted there intentionally or by accident? It's unclear.

For as long as there've been gardens, gardeners have pondered the epistemology of weeds.

Because a weed famously is defined by what it's not. A weed is just a plant growing where it's not wanted, right? A hardy plant with the tenacity to thrive, neglected, in inhospitable turf.

A weed competes for resources—for space, sunlight, and water—with more desirable, intentional plants. It provides shelter where pests can overwinter. Early-season weeds offer sustenance to sap-sucking aphids and other insects, enabling them to grow strong enough to attack your tomatoes when the time is right.

In the proper context a weed can be a tincture, or a tea, or the main ingredient in your pasta with wild ramp pesto. If it roots in the right place it can fix nitrogen in the soil or anchor unstable ground. In fact there's a famous story that the first life to return to east London after the devastation of the Blitz came in the form of weeds. According to Richard Mabey, author of the book *Weeds*, by the end of the war, braken carpeted the nave of St. James Cathedral and ragwort scrambled up London Wall. The spread of the lowly rosebay willow herb was so thick and rapid it was welcomed with the nickname "bombweed."

But what's a weed on land no one cares about? In the loose taxonomy of common weeds, railway weeds are their own lowly category: tenacious, craven plants that have staked a claim to the roughest, most embattled turf around. Yarrow and curly dock. Prostrate pigweed, Russian pigweed, rough and smooth. Spotted knapweed, hoary cress, western goat's beard, and toothed spurge. They all have names and properties, but in the ledger of urban improvement count for nothing.

Before construction started I walked the Bloomingdale Trail a lot, climbing the fence at Julia de Burgos Park over on Whipple and more often than not heading east. To the west, near where the tracks split at Ridgeway, vegetation gave way to a ground cover of small hostile rocks, and long-abandoned freight cars offered privacy for all manner of illicit human activities.

To the east, though, the path grew soft and lush, and where, from the street, the tracks seemed a dark mass of decaying concrete, from above they vibrated with the full flower of midsummer.

Accident or intention?

Seed or weed?

Which is better in the long run? Is it even possible to quantify their relative good? Intention builds bridges; accident coats them with rust. Intention drops bombs; accident turns the rubble green. Intention sows spinach; accident raises lamb's quarters instead.

But, wait a minute. Weeds grow from seeds, same as radishes. Lamb's quarters is just wild spinach. You can eat it, too, just as well.

My friend Amy used to live on Monticello, just south of the trail, and she swore for months that from her garden she could see trains passing by overhead. We scoffed. Those tracks haven't been used for years! She was seeing ghosts, we teased, and Amy's ghost train was a running refrain until, one day, I saw it, too—a freight train, real as steel, moving smoothly west.

I did some poking around and the most likely explanation is that the trains were delivering flour to a nearby industrial bakery that, though warned of the imminent redevelopment of the line, waited until the very last possible minute to make alternate shipping arrangements. The least likely, though most lovely, explanation is the story told by longtime trail neighbors, who swear that the circus used to use those tracks, sending carloads of animals toward the United Center, elephants and giraffes nodding to condo dwellers as they passed.

This, of course, is a fairy tale, though friends in the neighborhood swear to its truth. No record of the circus train exists with either the railway or the city. It turns out, in fact, that Amy's ghost train may have been delivering neither bread nor beasts. Rather, in order for Canadian Pacific to hold on to the air rights above the tracks all these years, they were required by law to keep them in use. And so every once in a while, for no reason, they'd run a train bearing nothing slowly by.

In April 2014 the Chicago Department of Transportation removed the old railway bridge at the Ashland Avenue end of the Bloomingdale Trail. It was taken to a work yard, scrubbed clean of rust, repainted, and then driven at dawn one mile west to Western, where it was reinstalled, and now connects the neighborhoods of Humboldt Park and Bucktown. The video of the bridge's slow, slow transit, available online, reminds me of footage of the journey of Michael Heizer's "Levitated Mass," the 350-ton granite boulder Heizer—a reclusive land artist perhaps best known for his 1970 earthwork "Double Negative"—had excavated from a Southern California quarry in 2012 and trucked over ten nights, at a stately two miles per hour, to the Los Angeles Museum of Contemporary Art.

Over those ten nights crowds of thousands gathered to marvel and clap, and others to mock and jeer. It's just a rock, the skeptics scoffed. Why waste all this time and money staking a claim to art? But like "Double Negative"—which is basically two big gashes cut into the earth atop a remote Nevada mesa—the appeal of the big rock, which now sits suspended above a deep trench cut into the LACMA plaza, is as much about what's not there as what is.

Weed or seed?

Can't a plant—a rock, a trail, a home—be both at once?

All summer long city crews have been working on the bridge supports at Humboldt Boulevard, spitting distance from my door, jackhammering away at the unhappy hour of 7:00 A.M. When this phase of construction is done, there'll be a new access ramp over on Whipple, and bleacher seating installed along the Humboldt overpass that will give visitors a place to sit and rest, and look down at traffic on the boulevard, and in my front yard.

It's a long arc to this yard from that first apartment on Augusta, the one that anchored me in Chicago. I was only there one year, but in the eighteen that have passed since I haven't strayed far from that central square, even as its perimeter has expanded, pushing past Western to California and beyond, and north to the edge of the Bloomingdale Trail, whose rocks and weeds inscribed new memories into my muscles as recently as last year.

I went up on the trail in July 2014, on a city-sanctioned tour organized for the neighbors. We had to wear hard hats and safety vests, but even so we didn't get far. It had rained all morning and the construction site above, invisible from the ground, was a dark, rutted moonscape of mud and debris, so violently at odds with the trail of memory that as I clambered back down the embankment I realized I was shaking, stunned into emotion.

According to the plan for the site, once construction is complete the trail will be home to an elaborate new ecosystem of native plants, with hanging gardens of forsythia, thickets of poplars and maidenhair ferns, and meadows of blue flax and bee balm, goat's beard and yellow mullein—desirable, intentional, weeds no more. A spiraling observatory—an earthwork built from soil and rubble—will anchor the western trailhead, its access points marked by evergreen spires. A tunnel of paperbark maples will open onto a public arts space at Ashland, and magnolias will bloom over Julia de Burgos Park.

Like the circus train, it will soon be a true-life fairy tale that once upon a time in the city you could climb a fence and take a long walk through nothing, along a trail of beautiful weeds.[13]

---

[13] The 606 trail opened in June 2015 to wide acclaim; a few months later, the land where the garden grew was sold to a developer. In the summer of 2017, the last of a set of five luxury townhomes was under construction on the site.

KATHRYN M. FLINN

This Is a Place

LIKE MANY TEENAGERS, I COULD not wait to leave the place where I grew up, in western Pennsylvania. There, my family often took a walk on a nearby Rails-to-Trails path that I liked to call the Trail of Ecological Destruction. This former railroad bed lined with invasive shrubs crosses creeks turned orange by acid mine drainage, passes the sewage treatment plant and the recycling center, and ends at a coal-fired power plant that releases more sulfur dioxide than any other power plant in the nation. I wanted to hike the Appalachian Trail, not this devastated landscape.

But, after years of working as an ecologist, I have come to realize that grim terrain like this holds endless ecological interest. I recently took a position as a biology professor near Cleveland, and I'm fully confident that ecological research in the immediate region can sustain a career's worth of curiosity. But I choose to do local ecology for another compelling reason—I have found that the local, lived-in landscape actually works best as a tool for helping people discover and value the environment. I do local ecology not because it's cheap, not because it's convenient, but because it has unique educational value.

Yet studying ecology in the Rust Belt clearly involves a public relations problem. Students, parents, administrators, and funders often fail to understand the appeal of local ecology. Even some ecologists, with their focus on biological diversity, tend to ignore the local in favor of places seen as globally significant or simply exotic. In fact, it is surprisingly easy to earn a biology degree without once interacting with organisms in a local habitat.

Any college worth its salt has a Study Abroad office. Just once, I would like to direct a student to the Study Our Home office. After all, the word "ecology" means the study of home. We have biology courses where students spend half a semester studying the natural history of Ecuador and half a semester photographing blue-footed boobies. What might happen if students spent an equal amount of time immersing themselves in their own landscapes?

To begin to focus attention on the local landscape, I realized that I needed to be able to recognize, articulate, and communicate the specific lessons of local ecology. What can students learn locally better than anywhere else? What exactly am I teaching when I teach ecology in urban wastelands, wetland restorations, the humblest of parks, or wherever is nearest to hand?

One late spring, I had planned a pollination ecology lab, but no native plants were flowering yet. So I took my students to a CVS parking lot, where a hedge of ornamental quince bushes had a pink riot of flowers mobbed by bees. After some urging, they set to work with their field notebooks, hand lenses, and butterfly nets. What is the difference if I teach pollination ecology in a rain forest in Costa Rica or in a CVS parking lot? Students learn the same observation skills and pollination ecology techniques. The same ecological principles pertain. The difference is that, to get to the rain forest, students must endure a six-hour flight and likely a harrowing bus ride. They must pay thousands of dollars and don their technical polyester zip-off pants. All of this communicates to them that what they are about to see is worth paying attention to. By teaching ecology in a CVS parking lot, I send the same message: This is a place worth noticing, a place of ecological interest.

The first lesson local ecology teaches is: Pay attention. Once I had a hundred-year-old holly tree in my urban front yard, but not until I did an assignment I had given my students did I learn about holly leaf miners. Apparently there are several species of insects whose whole life consists of making traces in holly leaves, and there are several scientists who have spent their careers figuring out this interaction. I went outside. Sure enough, my holly tree had them. Sharing the street with holly leaf miners made it look slightly different.

Last fall my students discovered a spectacularly armored wheel bug in an abandoned orchard behind a baseball field. They had no idea that something like a wheel bug could exist. Do they respect this place more, given the possibility of wheel bugs?

"Most of us are still related to our native fields as the navigator to undiscovered islands in the sea," Thoreau wrote late in life. "We can any afternoon discover a new fruit there, which will surprise us by its beauty or sweetness. So long as I saw in my walks one or two kinds of berries whose names I did not know, the proportion of the unknown seemed indefinitely, if not infinitely, great." In fact, none of us has the least idea what is going on under our noses. Geneticist Christopher Mason and his colleagues recently reported that almost half of the DNA they found in the New York City subway system was from organisms unknown to science. *The New York Times* quoted Mason as saying, "People don't look at a subway pole and think, 'It's teeming with life.' After this study, they may. But I want them to think of it the same way you'd look at a rain forest, and be almost in awe and wonder, effectively, that there are all these species present."

The second lesson: There is plenty left to discover, and you can start right here. Also, what you discover might change your mind.

Deep and inchoate ideas about how people interact with nature have a surprisingly strong influence on the teaching and learning of ecology. In his book *Thoreau's Country*, David Foster pointed out that when Thoreau built his cabin, the landscape around Walden Pond was extensively farmed, fenced, and populated. Diana Saverin recently noted in *The Atlantic* that while Annie Dillard wrote *Pilgrim at Tinker Creek*, she was a suburban housewife. Few people remember that Edward Abbey spent his formative years in western Pennsylvania, near the town of Home. These facts need to be emphasized because many implicitly assume that only an individual alone in the wilderness can experience nature. Is it any wonder children don't spend enough time experiencing nature in their backyards when parents hardly credit their backyards with offering an authentic experience of the natural world?

I might walk to work on the streets of Berea, Ohio, and daydream about building a cabin in Alaska or backpacking on the Pacific Crest Trail. Of course, there's nothing wrong

with valuing wilderness or visiting Alaska. But this thinking can demean my surroundings. There are probably plants
in the sidewalk cracks I can't identify yet.

If everywhere is nature, why not turn the question
around? What is the difference if I teach pollination ecology in the Costa Rican rain forest instead of the CVS parking lot? The difference, I think, is that we live here. Students
buy ramen noodles at this CVS. They are complicit in the
processes that led to the paving, the planting of ornamental
quince bushes, and the importing of European honeybees.
Whatever happens here, to the asphalt and the quinces and
the bees, they need to know about it, because they have to
live with it. As Thoreau exhorts in *Wild Fruits*, his belatedly
discovered final manuscript:

> *Do not think, then, that the fruits of New England are*
> *mean and insignificant while those of some foreign land*
> *are noble and memorable. Our own, whatever they may be,*
> *are far more important to us than any others can be. They*
> *educate us and fit us to live here in New England. Better for*
> *us is the wild strawberry than the pineapple, the wild apple*
> *than the orange, the chestnut and pignut than the cocoa-nut*
> *and almond, and not on account of their flavor merely, but*
> *the part they play in our education.*

Thoreau does not call wild strawberries "just as interesting" as pineapples. He does not say we could learn "just as
much" from our local fruits. He calls them "far more important to us"—specifically for their educational value. Local
fruits and local places teach us about our roles in nature—
not just as naturalists or scientists, but as parts of ecosys-

tems. The landscapes where we live are the ones we are most responsible for, and they teach us about the consequences of our actions.

My own sense of responsibility for the landscape where I grew up burgeoned when I learned how my ancestors had participated in shaping it. In the 1790s, my great-great-great-great-grandfather John McCullough bought 250 acres of forested land near Burnside, Pennsylvania, and spent the rest of his life clearing and farming it with his wife and twelve children. In 1880, his granddaughter Mollie married a logger, who also built things out of wood, especially wagons. Mollie's brother owned a sawmill, ran a lumber company, and opened a coal mine. Through the first decades of the 1900s, her daughter and son-in-law worked for a coal company. By the 1970s, my father was growing 20 million trees a year on farmland John McCullough and his neighbors had cleared. I grew up with young forests and orange creeks because my own family had created them. By teaching local ecology, I give students a similar sense: This is the place where we live, that we have shaped and continue to shape. This is the place where our children will live.

Ecologist Josh Donlan and other advocates of rewilding—especially reintroducing large carnivores—start from the premise that "earth is now nowhere pristine." They argue that because our actions affect every ecosystem on earth, we should claim this responsibility and manage ecosystems intentionally. Surely there are no better case studies in how human actions shape landscapes than the landscapes where we live. Certainly, educators need to help students make global connections—when they drive across campus instead of walking, they might contribute infinitesimally to a change in the mist regime of an epiphytic orchid in a rain forest canopy in Costa Rica. Interactions with our local landscapes are simply more immediate and concrete. When I take students in western Pennsylvania to compare invertebrate communities in streams with and without acid mine drainage, they understand the results within the context of their lives. They come from old company towns. Their uncles sell mining equipment. Their neighbors work for the power plant. They mountain bike on slag piles. And they like to fish. Doing local ecology provides a direct impetus to take ownership of our home landscapes, to accept our responsibility as stewards.

This third lesson is perhaps the greatest social benefit of local ecology: It is well to cultivate adults who can pay attention and continue to learn from nature. "Those who dwell, as scientists or laymen, among the beauties and mysteries of the earth, are never alone or weary of life," wrote Rachel Carson, who developed her sense of wonder in an industrial city near Pittsburgh. But as a society we also need citizens who take responsibility for the ways they interact with nature. This may be best learned through the intimate and practical interactions we can only have with the landscapes in which we live.

G. M. DONLEY

That Better Place; or, the Problem with Mobility

LOOK OUT THE WINDOW OF an airplane as you take off from just about any American city and you see a vast carpet of loosely woven streets and parking lots extending far from the city center, gradually disintegrating into loose threads at the fringe. The approach to most European cities, by contrast, is characterized by an abrupt shift from open farmland to the tight-knit tangle that characterizes places laid out before the rise of developers and highway planners, neighborhoods that grew organically based on how far people could walk.

Centuries ago, traveling great distances was slow and difficult—and often dangerous. For people who came to the American continent from far away, getting here entailed significant hardship. Think of traversing a tumultuous ocean in a leaky wooden ship full of rats to get to a vast wild continent with extreme weather and exciting new hazards like poison ivy and rattlesnakes. The heroic narrative of mobility had its evil counterpart as well: if you were brought to this hemisphere as a slave, that meant someone else had the power to control your movement. So it's no surprise that the freedom to move is an enduring aspect of American mythology.

But a funny thing has happened: the rise of increasingly

fast, safe, and affordable transportation over the past hundred years has made it so easy to move around that there really isn't any challenge or heroism to it anymore. Yet the psychological allure of going to a "Better Place" endures—whether one is migrating from one side of the country to another or between municipalities within a metro area. Mobility is romanticized throughout popular culture in everything from cowboy hats to road movies to every car ad you ever saw. For all its romantic appeal, though, there is also something less than noble about constant motion: for many Americans, the default response in a "fight or flight" situation has become the latter—run away. Welcome to the Land of the Free, Home of the [no longer at this address, skedaddled to the suburbs].

Easy mobility has made possible all kinds of things unimaginable a hundred years ago: living fifty miles from work and getting there in less than an hour; shipping fresh fruit from distant continents so regular folks can buy it cheap down the street at the discount store; flying from Detroit to Tokyo for a long weekend. But it has also created problems few foresaw. For one thing, though we may behave like nomads, we don't build like nomads. A highly mobile existence calls for tents and caravans, not bricks and mortar. But we still build for permanence. So whenever people decide it's time to go to a Better Place, they not only throw resources into new houses, roads, and businesses, they also abandon all the houses, roads, and businesses where they started out. What happens to all that stuff, all that investment?

The Rust Belt has proven to be an ideal laboratory for exploring the practical problems associated with a society habituated to easy mobility, specifically what results when mobility outruns population growth. Booming growth tends to mask economic and social side effects. But lucky us, we haven't had any booming growth for a while, so the results are plain to see here.

TOO MUCH RETAIL SPACE

In the early 1990s, a certain discount retailer erected a store in Cleveland Heights. Twenty years later, that same retailer put up a new, bigger store about half a mile away in the neighboring city of South Euclid, stomping out a former golf course in the process. The Cleveland Heights location was abandoned and remains a vacant hulk to this day.

Whenever this kind of thing happens, people talk about which city offered which tax credits, who was serious about being business friendly, which neighborhood is on the decline, *blah blah blah*. But more likely it's just that these buildings aren't made to last any longer than twenty years. Once the roof starts to leak and the parking lot is full of potholes, the owners more often than not just walk away from the thing rather than spending any money to fix it up, and write off the loss on the depreciated value to offset other profits. In other words, these may look kind of like buildings, but functionally they are tents—Sheetrock and metal-stud and particleboard tents pitched on concrete-slab ground cloths, taking up space that no one can use for anything else.

TOO MUCH HOUSING

Houses have generally been built for the longer haul. New people can move in and use them after the previous occupants leave. Urban planners describe a regional pattern of housing reuse as "filtering." The people who initially build homes and live in a city's earliest neighborhoods eventually move out for newer or bigger quarters and other people move in behind them. As those buildings get older, their relative value decreases, and the people moving into them correspondingly tend to be of somewhat lower income than the previous residents. The wealthiest people are generally building and moving into the newest buildings, while the poorest people are moving into the most affordable properties in the older areas—and in between, people are steadily "filtering" from lower value to higher value homes as they are able. It never happens quite that neatly, but that's the concept.

There's a functional elegance to this filtering scenario in that it provides housing for people at a wide range of incomes and allows for attainable step-ups to more expensive places as people are able to improve their lot economically and socially. And, in a cold Darwinian sort of way, it selects out the least viable structures, while buildings that have more inherent quality tend to get more attention and retain more value even as they age.

The functional elegance has run into some inelegant dysfunction in the Rust Belt, however, because for the filtering mechanism to work well there must be steady population growth. When population growth stops but building continues, two things start happening right away: the number of abandoned properties goes up as people "filter" out of the worst housing, and overall property values go down due to the market oversupply that outpaces regional demand. The depressed values further discourage investment in the upkeep of the lower-end properties, which accelerates the decline in real estate values.

STRESSED TAX BASES

Because schools and city services are typically funded through property and income taxes, a decline in relative property value and average income means either that municipalities need to increase tax rates to generate the per-household dollar amount needed to sustain services at historic levels, or those services need to be cut, or some of each.

Some communities can deal with that—they understand that their higher tax rate still translates to a reasonable tax bill for a house of a given size when compared to the newer places (which charge a lower tax rate on a house that costs more per square foot to get a similar dollar amount). This is why people happily still choose to live in places like Cleveland Heights, Shaker Heights, and Lakewood in the Cleveland area even though tax rates have crept up over the decades: the total cost of a mortgage plus taxes is still favorable compared to that of outlying areas, and the inner-ring lifestyle simply does not exist out there. This isn't specifically a Rust Belt phenomenon, but an age-of-housing phenomenon: nationwide, older homes tend to have lower per-square-foot property costs and higher property tax rates than newer ones. But in a high-mobility/low-growth scenario such has characterized the Rust Belt since the 1970s, some areas of a city lose so much value so quickly and so pervasively that there seems to be no way out of it except to let things crumble and start over.

The inequities and waste are further exacerbated when the region is a patchwork of small, competing municipalities rather than one geographically big city. It's hard to sell independent municipalities on the concept of some kind of regional cost sharing when many of them were created specifically *not* to share with their neighbors, but rather to keep their own costs low while enjoying the spillover value of being near an urban economic center.

Overbuilding is all the more of a drag in places like Cleveland or Detroit or Buffalo or Toledo where there is still ample and relatively inexpensive green space to expand into on the outskirts, because every new project saddles the region not only with excess housing and retail capacity but also with the long-term burden of sustaining exponentially more infrastructure. In geographically constrained places, people end up redeveloping underused spaces within the city because there is less blank space outside it to sprawl into.[14]

PERSISTENT SEGREGATION

When these mobility patterns are layered on top of a legacy of discrimination, we get typical Rust Belt racial and economic segregation. Recently a couple of items have made the rounds of the internet showing the geographic distribution of people by race and income in the U.S. By some of

---

[14] Thomas Bier, senior fellow at the Levin College of Urban Affairs at Cleveland State University, has written numerous articles about these patterns in the Cleveland area: http://www.cleveland.com/opinion/index .ssf/2015/08/ohio_policies_encouraging_the.html

these measures, Cleveland is the most segregated city in the country.[15] Notably, a number of the other most segregated cities on that list have similar histories of regional population stagnation or shrinkage since the late 1960s.

Beginning in the 1930s or earlier in Cleveland and many other cities, properties were designated as the lowest investment quality, based, presumably, on age and location. This designation seems to have established a decades-long trajectory. A 2014 *Belt* feature showed that much of East Cleveland was designated as the lowest, "grade D" property many decades before the notorious years of white flight[16] in the 1960s. Those old redlines set in motion a sequence of events that helped define the current segregation of Cleveland: in part because investment in upkeep was discouraged by the low rating, many grade D properties steadily lost value leading up to the 1960s. Wealthier residents moved out and were replaced by people of lesser means. Many of the new residents were renters because banks would not issue mortgages due to the low investment grade. Discriminatory renting, lending, and selling practices prevented black families from moving into any places except for these lowest-grade neighborhoods, which meant that even if a family managed to buy a home, often the property did not increase in value, so little if any wealth was accumulated, resulting in some geographic areas that were disproportionately populated by people with low wealth and dark skin.

By the time black families were able to move relatively

---

[15] http://www.huffingtonpost.com/entry/the-9-most-segregated-cities-in-america_us_55df53e9e4b0e7117ba92d7f

[16] http://beltmag.com/the-legacy-of-redlining-in-rust-belt-cities

freely after the civil rights advances of the 1960s, the region had already entered its post-industrial population decline, which meant there was very little demand pressure for anyone of any race to move into the older, deteriorated neighborhoods. So most of the acres of land that were segregated and low-income fifty years ago have remained segregated and low-income. Meanwhile, the number of people living in those neighborhoods has declined precipitously. The Cleveland neighborhood of Hough claimed 72,000 people and was predominantly black in 1960; by the year 2000 it was still predominantly black but had less than 20,000 residents. (Granted, there is some upbeat news in that downward trend: many of the African Americans who moved out are now a generation or two into a more prosperous life in racially integrated places.)

A fascinating visual data project by the Cooper Center plots the residence location of every single person in the United States, broken down in broad categories by race, and it shows this phenomenon dramatically. Looking at the entire United States, it's clear that the relatively few people who live in vast, sparsely populated rural areas are overwhelmingly white (with the exception of some rural areas of the Southeast that have more black residents), while all other races are concentrated in urban areas. If you were to draw borders around those large areas where the very few humans are white, and then filled each entire area with a solid color indicating the predominant skin color of the residents, it would appear that the United States is 90 percent white. Many of the geographic segregation maps are drawn this way—this area is white, this area is Asian, this area is black, this area is Hispanic—but it doesn't show if there are fifty people per acre or one person per square mile. Acres aren't people. The dot map shows that some areas of greater Cleveland (especially the inner suburbs on both sides of town) are pretty well mixed in race and income, but the amount of land occupied by those places is modest compared to the amount of land occupied by population-depleted inner-city areas and especially the sparsely populated, mostly white outer suburbs and countryside. Because the actual number of people is so few, any influx of diverse population into these geographic areas would quickly change the picture of segregation—however, there has been no influx of anyone into those inner-city neighborhoods for a good sixty years.

SCHOOL RATINGS AS REAL ESTATE MARKETING TOOLS

Another realm in which the dynamics of mobility operate is in our schools and the tools we use to rate them. In Ohio, the primary effect of the state's student-testing regime has not been to improve educational outcomes, but to encourage migration within regions. The test methodology is designed so that the reports don't show which districts are making the most difference but rather which ones start off with the highest-achieving students.

The design of a research instrument usually says a lot about the motivations of its designers, and it would appear from this example that the primary purpose of the state report cards is to spur economic development in some places at the expense of other places. Why else would you take the valuable precise individual student test data you have about how James is doing in reading and Jasmine is doing in math and then throw away the value by unscientifically lumping scores together to make contests between communities, unless the primary goal is to get people to desire one community over another? If your motivation were really to help those individual students, you'd use the individual test data to identify which students need what help, and help them.

But the "school versus school" mentality promoted by the state report cards is pervasive. Currently in Ohio, some politicians continue to discuss plans whereby funding could "follow the student." A kid who is doing poorly could go to a different school and state funds attached to that kid would go to the new school. This proposal plays right into the "fight or flight" mentality, too, as it presumes that the solution to every problem is for the individual to move.

Given the system we have had, it is utterly unsurprising that we don't see overall statewide improvement in student performance, but we do see families abandoning some communities to move to other communities in response to the school report cards. If getting people to move is our goal, we could save everyone a lot of trouble simply by telling those folks to look at income levels. Just go to Wikipedia and look up the wealthiest cities in Ohio. Pick out the top twenty wealthiest places in the greater Cleveland area. Now go look up the top ten highest-scoring Cleveland-area school districts. Those ten school districts cover all but two of the twenty wealthiest places.

Clearly, using student test data to set up a contest among school districts does little more than magnify the advantage of communities that are already advantaged. Worse than that, it's not telling us anything we didn't already know decades ago. Wealthier kids have a starting gate that is much closer to the finish line. Everybody loves a horse race, but there's no drama to this one. Just give them the roses at the beginning and don't waste our time and money staging a rigged contest.

FIVE STEPS

Certainly there are other unintended negative consequences of easy mobility that merit attention, but these five— abandoned crappy retail space, too much housing, stressed tax bases, persistent racial segregation, and the use of schools as real estate marketing—give us plenty to chew on. It's not surprising that our cities have run into unforeseen side effects of increased mobility: society has never encountered these conditions and possibilities before. But now that we've seen what's going on, maybe we could make some adjustments so that the mobility-driven evolution of our cities isn't quite so brutal to individuals and so disruptive to regional economies. The problems are complex, of course, but still, each of the five ailments above might respond to a fairly simple treatment.

RETAIL: LEAVE NO TRACE

There is a principle taught to every Boy Scout: leave no trace. No responsible camper would just leave a worn-out tent in the woods for someone else to clean up. But that is exactly the behavior of big-box retailers. This is frustrating because it comes so close to a sensible approach: why not just acknowledge that big-box retail is nomadic and build things in such a manner that they can be easily dismantled and either transported to a new site or recycled? Maybe the town where the retailer has built charges a deposit that would cover the cost of putting the land back the way it was and the occupant doesn't get their deposit back if they don't restore the place to the way they found it. If an old "box" is vacant for more than a year, it has to come down. Packing up camp is part of the process, just like setting it up.

New construction on blank land enjoys a lot of subsidies, from the roads that literally pave the way, to the utility lines paid for by past customers, to tax structures that reward new construction over the maintenance or rehabilitation of existing houses. The people building new on the outskirts are among the most advantaged already, so they really don't need the less wealthy people of the region to subsidize them. We can probably eliminate those discounts. If the lack of a new-construction discount leads someone to decide to stay put and upgrade an existing structure rather than building new, that's a pretty good sign that building new was not really an economically sound idea in the first place. Over the years, the accumulation of such decisions would gradually mitigate the housing oversupply.

TAX BASE: REDUCE OVERSUPPLY AND DON'T PENALIZE REINVESTMENT

Broad-based regional tax and revenue sharing is probably unrealistic in an intentionally balkanized place like greater Cleveland, but it might be possible to assess a modest fee on new construction whose sole purpose is to fund the demolition of abandoned housing at the same rate that new units are added relative to population (that is, if housing occupancy is growing at the same rate as new construction, then there's no fee). That would help keep a lid on the oversupply of housing, thus keeping real estate values up across the region, and it would rid older areas of dangerous, blighted structures, and prime those areas for quicker redevelopment.

Americans are conditioned from birth to complain about taxes, but it isn't necessarily a problem that older areas have higher tax rates, because the older real estate is more affordable in the first place. However, what if you want to build a new house at $150 or $200 per square foot in an old neighborhood whose higher tax rates assume a $75-square-foot value because most buildings have already depreciated for ninety years? Yikes! Older towns need to encode utterly predictable graduated abatements that make the effective tax rate on new construction or extensive renovation in inner-ring Cleveland Heights the same as it would be for new construction in exurban Macedonia (and they need to widely publicize this standard abatement). The city will do fine because the per-square-foot value of the new construction is higher than the typical older Cleveland Heights home, and thus roughly the same dollar amount will come in each year. Similar abatements should apply to any major investment in a home's infrastructure that bring its systems up to "contemporary" standards. Measures such as these would encourage reinvestment in these older neighborhoods, where much of the highest-quality (if older) housing stock already exists. Such reinvestment would be a net gain for the region.

Finally, some real estate appraisers and bankers use a set of methods incorporating an assumed "rot rate" that can define entire neighborhoods as bad investments if they are over fifty or even thirty years old. Such formulas exist because they make it easy for lenders to make decisions—just like those property ratings from the 1930s made it easy. But easy isn't the same as fair or smart. Lenders and appraisers need to account for the fact that houses originally built for middle- and upper-middle-class owners between about 1890 and 1940 have some of the highest-quality construction and materials even though some formulas might suggest they are past their economic lifespan. Nothing built since then can compete with the level of handcraftsmanship that went into a regular middle-class house. And those houses are tough— the structural wood in the pre-dimension lumber days was notably stronger than post–World War II product (just try to saw through an old joist). The scale of the neighborhoods built in that era was defined by the streetcar and the early days of the automobile: notably more spacious than earlier in the nineteenth century and designed to allow for cars, but still compact enough to comfortably get around on foot or by bicycle. These are the authentic neighborhoods upon which "New Urbanism" is modeled, and these factors of crafts-manship and neighborhood form should enhance invest-ment value—not only for those houses built 80 to 120 years ago, but for any new construction that embodies high craft, quality materials, and efficient site design.

SEGREGATION: REIMAGINE IDENTITY

Round one in the growth of Cleveland's population was usu-ally a story of ethnically homogenous groups coming here and setting up ethnically homogenous enclaves (by choice or not). Yes, the city contained diverse cultures, but at closer magnification one could see that these groups did not mix a whole lot at the neighborhood level.

But that seems to be changing now—as downtown, Ohio City, and University Circle attract new investment and new population, property values are climbing in those areas and in nearby neighborhoods.[17] The demographic makeup of those growing core areas tends to be fairly diverse, and one can expect that as population growth spreads outward from those centers, the people occupying the formerly segregated adjacent land will be increasingly mixed in race and culture as well. Places like these can provide a model for how empowering it is for a community to see itself not just through a monocle of common heritage, but through a multidimensional sense of community and shared values. If the coming years show significant population growth in the city, it will be the first time in Cleveland's history that city neighborhoods have grown without an official framework of racial segregation, and we ought to make the most of that opportunity.

It's worth noting as well that for every Shaker Heights that successfully integrated in the 1960s and '70s, there are also places that "flipped" from white to black well after the civil rights era, not because of any racist legal framework, but because of the prejudices and fears of individual home- and business owners. As long as we continue to see each other and ourselves mainly through the lens of race, then we will continue to sort neighborhoods by race. The only

17 http://www.cleveland.com/chagrin-falls/index.ssf/2015/09/chagrin
_valley_home_values_are.html

way to get beyond that is to cultivate other senses of shared identity that we decide are more important.

SCHOOLS: LOCAL CONTROL WITH STATE SUPPLEMENT

For more than a century, schools have been strongly identified with the communities they serve—not only in the rah-rah sense of cheering for the hometown sports team, but also in the civic significance and permanence that is signaled by stately architecture and the usually prominent location of the high school in a spacious setting at some kind of focal point of the town. This is all great, but it poses a problem in the context of statewide standards: this local tradition can sometimes confound the state's avowed interest in providing something that approaches fair opportunity in education for all students.

Shifting the way tests are used could not only help improve educational outcomes but at the same time allow each local district to retain some local flavor. First, let each district fund itself as it chooses, and let each substantially control its methods to best match its local community. Second, the state should use its test data to improve education where the need is greatest, on a student-by-student basis. That could be as simple as having state-employed specialists trained in remediating particular kinds of learning deficits—in reading, writing, math, science, history, arts, and so on—come in to supplement the local school's own teaching corps. Certainly that's a more effective response than saying, "We're going to publish school district report cards that reflect where the rich and poor kids live and you can try to move to a wealthier place—and good luck with that."

SHOULD I STAY OR SHOULD I GO?

Fear of retail competition, fear of a home investment losing value, fear of taxes rising, fear of other races, fear that your kids might fall behind other kids—our preoccupation with mobility seems driven as much by fear as by romance. These days it's not so much fear of oppression or persecution but fear of being left behind in a policy environment that favors flight and abandonment, that privileges those with the wealth and inclination to move. It can even start to seem as if this policy environment might not be an accident—that it is an intentional effort to make sure the advantaged can always leave behind the disadvantaged. But that would only happen if these policies were crafted by people who already had most of the wealth and power and felt entitled to even more. And that would never happen, would it?

So let's be nice and assume the policies weren't created with our current result in mind, but that the set of assumptions that underpinned those policies haven't held true in the Rust Belt and we've had unintended consequences. The primary faulty assumption has been that population would continue to grow. When you combine subsidized residential mobility with flat or shrinking population, you get rising taxes, property depreciation, and economic stagnation, and all the social ills associated with those stresses.

But of course regions do go through cycles of growth and shrinkage, so it makes sense to question the assumption that mobility is the solution to every problem. In our Rust Belt scenario of regional population stagnation, a romanticized devotion to mobility has often caused more problems than it has solved. Desegregation was made possible by greater mobility. And suburban flight to escape school busing was also made possible by mobility.

All of that said, sometimes flight *is* the smart response. Sometimes moving to another place is the best way to "reset" a student's approach to school. Sometimes a simple change of scenery opens up one's mind to new possibilities and helps to shed old negative expectations. An August 24, 2015, *New Yorker* article by Malcolm Gladwell described a study by the University of Oxford's David Kirk that compared the recidivism rates for prisoners who were in a Louisiana penitentiary during Hurricane Katrina. Many of their home neighborhoods were destroyed by the storm, so when they were eventually released from prison, some had to relocate to other places while others went back to their old neighborhoods. The ones who went back to the old neighborhoods had a 60 percent recidivism rate, while for those who went to other places it was 45 percent. Human behavior is shaped not just by the inclinations of the individual, but by social settings that reinforce or discourage particular actions.

Of course that's also the thinking behind the breakup of concentrated poverty that was embodied in high-rise housing projects by tearing down the housing and dispersing former residents throughout a region. Statistics show that such measures have decreased crime and increased opportunity for many of the people who had lived in the projects. But that doesn't mean all neighbors are eager for Section 8 housing on their own street (all those old fears at play). The people who have most exploited mobility have not been those whom it would most benefit (people stuck in toxic poor neighborhoods) but the wealthier half of society using their money to distance themselves from poverty, and all too often that pattern of flight has had negative effects on the regional economy, not to mention the social fabric.

The view from the airplane makes it clear that in trying to spread too far too quickly, we weaken our very fabric— not only is it frayed at the edges, it's also unraveling in the middle. Flying into a Rust Belt city, you'll often see the blue sparkles of swimming pools giving way to cast-off neighborhoods left to rot as if they were fast-food trash tossed out the car window. We may be able to drive around that on the ground, but from the air it is plain to see that we are not only allowing weak places to compromise the structural integrity of the whole, but we are also missing an enormous opportunity to revive the existing fabric with new designs and stronger material. In our age of easy mobility, it's always an option to set out for what we imagine is that Better Place. But we might be smarter to invest where we are to make our place better.

Leaving and Staying

SALLY ERRICO

Losing Lakewood

I MOVED TO LAKEWOOD, OHIO, a few weeks after breaking up with my boyfriend and, not coincidentally, a few weeks after I started sleeping with Adam. My boyfriend and I had lived together on Cleveland's east side—his native stomping ground—and as soon as the first winter had hit, I had become desperate to leave.

"You realize the snowbelt that goes all the way to Buffalo starts here, right? Like, specifically *here*. If we lived twenty minutes west, we'd have an entirely different climate."

"I like the east side," he'd said. "Now hand me the ice scraper."

There were other reasons for moving to Lakewood. It seemed to me a city in the best possible ways: progressive in both its politics and its society, a place where a proud Cleveland met a youthful liberalism. It was full of shops and restaurants and bars, and their interconnectedness—the sheer number of them and their proximity to one another, and to residential streets, and to Cleveland itself—was to me a characteristic of what urban life should be.

On a more practical level, Lakewood was also where Adam lived.

I met him at a party in December, and when he mentioned that he and his girlfriend would be moving in together in May, I thought, *I have six months to make you fall in love with me.* I had known him for an hour.

The intensity of my attraction was unlike anything I'd ever felt: he was tall, slim, and impeccably dressed, with curly brown hair and eyes so dark they were almost black. As we got to know each other better over the next few months, I also discovered he was sometimes vain. He could be jealous and resentful. But his flaws made him more appealing, which is why I maintain that my attraction wasn't just physical. I was in love.

The situation was complicated by 1) my boyfriend and 2) Adam's girlfriend. For a while, I imagined that Adam and I could just . . . hang out together forever, complacent in our respective relationships, no rocking of boats. We had mutual friends, so there was always an excuse to see each other; we enjoyed the same things, so if we happened to find ourselves at, say, the same concert, hey, what a coincidence! But then one night, after we attended a wine-fueled fund-raiser for the Cleveland Public Theatre, he kissed me. I was living in Lakewood by the end of the month.

I found my apartment by driving around and looking for FOR RENT signs in the windows of buildings (it was a kinder, simpler, realty app–free time: 2004). I checked out houses, duplexes, and apartment complexes, some near the lake and others closer to the airport, some beautiful and others one leak away from being condemned. When I called the number in the window of a building on the corner of Detroit and Riverside, the owner said he could show me a one-bedroom immediately—he was there now, renovating it. For $525 a month, it was mine.

The neighborhood was everything. I could go to the dry cleaner and the liquor store *on the same walk*. Sushi, falafel, and pizza were just a short drive up Detroit. And if funds were low, so were prices at Marc's, that T.J. Maxx of food, with its dented tuna cans and inexplicably large selection of peanut butter. Stores and restaurants flew rainbow flags year-round, and the one business I knew of that was openly homophobic—a taxidermy shop that appeared closed even when it was open and had a bumper sticker reading GOD MADE ADAM AND EVE, NOT ADAM AND STEVE in the window—was also openly mocked. I could go for a morning run in the Metropark, and in the evening, have a glass of wine at Three Birds. By comparison, my hometown near Cedar Point had not one single store at which to buy a CD, and there was opposition to plans for a Taco Bell because the locals believed it would attract gangs. Lakewood was a Shangri-La.

And just off of Detroit: Adam's apartment, the seat of both my joy and misery. He hadn't broken up with his girlfriend yet, but soon, I just knew, it would happen. They'd never have the chance to move in together. In the meantime, my plan was simple: continue sleeping with him and wait for him to give in to our obvious chemistry. But I'd forget this on the days I'd drive past his street on my way home from work and see his girlfriend's car parked in front of his building. *Her carrrrrrr!* I would be in agony as I pulled into my parking lot, imagining them in a Kama Sutra's worth of positions—or worse, doing something like making dinner, throwing little puffs of flour at each other and laughing, a scene straight out of some stupid romantic comedy. I'd drag myself up the stairs of my building, collapsing in tears on the slipcovered couch that had been a hand-me-down from my grandparents.

This, as it turns out, is not a way to build self-esteem. I recognized that I'd become the kind of woman I'd always pitied, the "crazy" one waiting for a kind word or sign of affection from an emotionally (and otherwise) unavailable man. But I didn't know how to break out. I'd decide that I was done, that I was too disgusted with myself to continue, and I'd go on dates with other guys. But then Adam would call, and the adrenaline would flood me.

Complete escape seemed the only option. For years, I'd entertained the fantasy of moving to New York City—a giant Lakewood!—and I began to plan in earnest. But really, it was both a distraction and a bluff: I was sure Adam would stop me. Our relationship wasn't just sex, after all. We'd been friends before we'd been anything, and we'd spent nights talking about our lives, our ambitions, our secrets. That had to count for something.

I packed my apartment slowly, waiting. He never came. I got in the van and left Lakewood, this time by taking Detroit across the bridge and into Rocky River. I didn't want to drive down the streets we'd walked, or pass the diner where we'd sat across from each other in squeaky vinyl booths, talking over coffee until 4:00 A.M. More than anything, I didn't want to see his building. I felt at the time that he had taken Lakewood from me, but now, of course, I understand that I was the thief, and a cowardly one at that. I was leaving the only apartment I'd ever have that would be just mine: no roommates, no boyfriends. I'd been too obsessed with my heartbreak to allow myself the pleasure of being a single twenty-four-year-old woman in a city that I loved.

I later learned that Adam's girlfriend had been cheating on him all along. They had broken up right around the time I'd settled in New York, where every street had been full of things I wanted to tell him about and every face was that of a stranger.

MARGARET SULLIVAN

Notes from the Expatriate Underground

WE WERE SO TIRED OF those people—the ones who had moved away from Buffalo, but still wanted to lay claim to it. The ones who gathered at Buffalo taverns in various cities to cheer (or grieve) the Bills, but didn't have to think about the rusting steel mills along Route 5, or the problems of the second poorest city in the United States, or the constant infighting on the school board.

Although we true Buffalo people—the ones who actually lived in the Queen City—welcomed them back, with wan smiles, on the Wednesday nights before Thanksgiving, on Elmwood or Chippewa, we didn't think for a minute that they were really Buffalo People.

No, they were poseurs, in their "City of No Illusions" T-shirts, swigging Genny Cream Ale and debating the virtues of wings at Duff's versus Anchor Bar. Because after the holiday, or the wedding, or whatever had brought them back for a few days, they were gone, and we were here.

Still here.

I tolerated them for years, for decades. Now, I'm one of them: a Buffalo expatriate. And now, finally, I get it: the constant craving for the hometown, the need to talk about it all the time, the nostalgia for what was left behind.

I left for New York City in 2012, after most of a lifetime in Buffalo, including thirteen years as chief editor of the *Buffalo News*, where I had come as a summer intern after college in Washington and graduate school in Chicago. Three decades, somehow, went by. Parents died, children were born and raised. Then a job at *The New York Times* beckoned.

Now, after four years in Manhattan, I live in Washington, DC. These cities have their wonders, no doubt—glamour, spectacle, a sense of importance and being at the center of the world.

But so far, I haven't found anything as real as the First Friday fish fry at St. Mark's parish in north Buffalo. Or the Turkey Trot as a crucial calorie-burner before the big meal of the year. Or the first warm day of the spring when Delaware Park is alive with runners, tennis players, would-be hoop stars, and toddlers in strollers.

And that sense of place—that authenticity—is why we expatriates hold on so tight.

It's why we gather together in other places—for example, in a Buffalo bar in Sarasota, Florida, to watch the Bills get crushed on their overseas road game in London. Or why we gravitate to other Buffalo people who have made the same move. When I moved to New York City, I found a group of literary women with western New York ties; we called ourselves the Buffalo Gals, and met monthly for dinners to speculate on such matters as whether the Peace Bridge had been lit purple for Prince's death or for Queen

Elizabeth's birthday, and to talk about the accumulated snowfall in the Southern Tier.

It's also why Tim Russert, who grew up in south Buffalo, never stopped mentioning Buffalo sports teams when he was the host of NBC's *Meet the Press*. It's why Lauren Belfer, the novelist who wrote the Buffalo-based *City of Light*, comes to her hometown so often to speak to groups as varied as the working-class patrons of the Tonawanda Public Library and the white-gloved ladies of the Twentieth Century Club and the hipsters of Larkin Square. And it's why I've been so happy to write book reviews for the *Buffalo News*, and to come around every summer to delight, from a kayak, as the late-afternoon sunlight sparkles upon beautiful Lake Erie.

In short, we want the connection. We need the connection.

And while we know that this yearning may seem, to you who shovel the snow and pay the real estate taxes, like the passing interest of a mere dilettante—you may even feel it has a whiff of condescension—we must beg your indulgence.

Allow us expatriates to lay claim to the Buffalo that forged us and that sustains us. Because we frankly aren't sure who we would be without it. Without those roots grounding us and feeding us, we might wither away altogether.

So when we come around for the Wednesday night before Thanksgiving, or for the Fourth of July family reunion, or for our best friend's wedding reception at the Historical Society, we'll be listening for the words we want to hear.

Even if you deliver the phrase with an invisible roll of your eyes, please say it: "Welcome home."

JASON SEGEDY

Confessions of a Rust Belt Orphan; or, How I Learned to Stop Worrying and Love Akron

Go to sleep, Captain Future, in your lair of art deco
You were our pioneer of progress, but tomorrow's been
*   postponed*
Go to sleep, Captain Future, let corrosion close your eyes
If the board should vote to restore hope, we'll pass along the lie.
                                        —"CAPTAIN FUTURE," *The Secret*
                                                Sound of the NSA

IN THE BEGINNING . . .

As near as I can tell, the term "Rust Belt" originated some-time in the mid-1980s. That sounds about right.

I originated slightly earlier, in 1972, at St. Thomas Hospital in Akron, Ohio, Rubber Capital of the World. My very earliest memory is of a day, sometime in the summer of 1975, that my parents, my baby brother, and I went on a camping trip to Lake Milton, just west of Youngstown. I was three years old. To this day, I have no idea why, of all of the things that I could remember, but don't, I happen to remember this one. But it is a good place to start.

The memory is so vivid that I can still remember looking

at the green overhead freeway signs along the West Expressway in Akron. Some of the signs were in kilometers as well
as in miles back then, due to an ill-fated attempt to convert
Americans to the metric system in the 1970s. I remember the
overpoweringly pungent smell of rubber wafting from the
smokestacks of BFGoodrich and Firestone. I recall asking my
mother about it, and her explaining that those were the factories where the tires, and the rubber, and the chemicals were
made. They were made by hardworking, good people—people
like my uncle Jim. But more on that later.

When I was a little bit older, I would learn that this was
the smell of good jobs; of hard, dangerous work; and of the
way of life that built the modern version of this quirky and
gritty town. It was the smell that tripled Akron's population
between 1910 and 1920, transforming it from a sleepy former
canal town to the thirty-second largest city in America. It is
a smell laced with melancholy, ambivalence, and nostalgia—
for it was the smell of an era that was quickly coming to an
end (although I was far too young to be aware of this fact at
the time). It was sometimes the smell of tragedy.

We stopped by my grandparents' house, in Firestone Park,
on the way to the campground. I can still remember my
grandmother giving me a box of Barnum's Animal Crackers
for the road. She was always kind and generous like that.

Who were my grandparents? My grandparents were Akron. It's as simple as that. Their story was Akron's story. My
grandfather, George Segedy, was born in 1916, in Barnesboro,
a small coal-mining town in western Pennsylvania, somewhere among Johnstown, DuBois, and nowhere. His father, a
coal miner, had emigrated there from Hungary nine years
earlier. My grandmother, Helen Szabo, was born in Barber-

ton, Ohio, in 1920. Barberton was reportedly the most indus-
trialized city in the United States, per capita, at some point
around that time.

They were both factory workers for their entire working
lives (I don't think they called jobs like that "careers" back
then). My grandfather worked at the Firestone Tire and
Rubber Company. My grandmother worked at Saalfield
Publishing, a factory that was one of the largest producers
of children's books, games, and puzzles in the world. Today,
both of the plants where they worked form part of a gutted,
derelict, post-apocalyptic moonscape in south Akron, located
between that same West Expressway and perdition. The City
of Akron has plans for revitalizing this former industrial area.
It needs to happen, but there are ghosts there.

> My name is Ozymandias, King of Kings,
> Look on my works, ye Mighty, and despair!
> Nothing beside remains. Round the decay
> Of that colossal wreck, boundless and bare
> The lone and level sands stretch far away.
>
> —"OZYMANDIAS," PERCY BYSSHE SHELLEY

My grandparents' house exemplified what it was to live in
working-class Akron in the late 1970s and early 1980s. My
stream-of-consciousness memories of that house include: lots
of cigarettes and ashtrays; *Hee Haw*; *The Joker's Wild*; fresh
tomatoes and peppers; Fred and Lamont Sanford; Archie
and Edith Bunker; Herb Score and Indians baseball on the
radio on the front porch; hand-knitted afghans; cold cans
of Coca-Cola and Pabst Blue Ribbon; the Ohio Lottery;
chicken and galuskas (dumplings); a garage door that you

could eat off of; a meticulously maintained fourteen-year-old Chrysler with 29,000 miles on it; a refrigerator in the dining room because the kitchen was too small; catching fireflies in jars; and all being right with the world.

I always associate the familiar comfort of that tiny two-bedroom bungalow with the omnipresence of cigarette smoke and television. I remember sitting there on May 18, 1980. It was my eighth birthday. We were sitting in front of the TV, watching coverage of the Mount St. Helens eruption in Washington state. I remember talking about the fact that it was going to be the year 2000 (the Future!) in just twenty years. I remember thinking about the fact that I would be twenty-eight years old then, and how inconceivably distant it all seemed. Things seem so permanent when you're eight, and time moves ever so slowly.

More often than not, when we visited my grandparents, my uncle Jim and aunt Helen would be there. Uncle Jim was born in 1936, in West Virginia. His family, too, had come to Akron to find work that was better paying, steadier, and less dangerous than the work in the coal mines. Uncle Jim was a rubber worker, first at Mohawk Rubber and then later at BFGoodrich. Uncle Jim also cut hair over at the most appropriately named West Virginia Barbershop, on South Arlington Street in east Akron. He was one of the best, most decent, kindest people whom I have ever known.

I remember asking my mother once why Uncle Jim never washed his hands. She scolded me, explaining that he did wash his hands, but that because he built tires, his hands were stained with carbon black, which wouldn't come out no matter how hard you scrubbed. I learned later that it would take about six months for that stuff to leach out of your pores once you quit working.

Uncle Jim died in 1983, killed in an industrial accident on the job at BFGoodrich. He was only forty-seven. The plant would close for good about a year later.

It was an unthinkably tragic event, at a singularly traumatic time for Akron. It was the end of an era.

TIMES CHANGE

My friend Della Rucker wrote a great post titled "The Elder Children of the Rust Belt," over at her blog, *Wise Economy*. It dredged up all of these old memories, and it got me thinking about childhood, about this place that I love, and about the experience of growing up just as an economic era (perhaps the most prosperous and anomalous one in modern history) was coming to an end.

That is what the late 1970s and early 1980s was: the end of one thing, and the beginning of (a still yet-to-be-determined) something else. I didn't know it at the time, but that's because I was just a kid.

In retrospect it was obvious: the decay, the deterioration, the decomposition, the slow-at-first-then-faster-than-you-can-see-it unwinding of an industrial machine that had been wound up far, far too tight. The machine runs until it breaks down, then it is replaced with a new and more efficient one—a perfectly ironic metaphor for an industrial society that killed the goose that laid the golden egg. It was a machine made up of unions, and management, and capitalized sunk costs, and supply chains, and commodity prices, and globalization.

Except it wasn't really a machine at all. It was really just people. And people aren't machines. When they are treated as such, and then discarded as obsolete, there are consequences. You could hear it in the music: from the decadent, desperately-seeking-something (escape) pulse of disco, to the (first) nihilistic and (then) fatalistic sound of punk and post-punk. It's not an accident that a band called Devo came from Akron, Ohio. De-evolution: the idea that instead of evolving, mankind has actually regressed, as evidenced by the dysfunction and herd mentality of American society. It sounded a lot like Akron in the late 1970s. It still sounds a little bit like the Rust Belt today.

As an adult, looking back at the experience of growing up at that time, you realize how much it colors your thinking and outlook on life. It's all the more poignant when you realize that the "end of an era" is never really an "end" as such, but is really a transition to something else. But to what, exactly?

The end of that era, which was marked by strikes, layoffs, and unemployment, was followed by its echoes and repercussions—economic dislocation, outmigration, poverty, and abandonment—as well as the more intangible psychological detritus: the pains from the phantom limb long after the amputation, the vertiginous sensation of watching someone (or something) die.

But it is both our tragedy and our glory that life goes on.

Della raised a lot of these issues in her post: our generation's ambivalent relationship with the American Dream (like Della, I feel the same unpleasant taste of rust in my mouth whenever I write or utter that phrase); our distrust of organizations and institutions; and our realization that you have to keep going, fight, and survive, in spite of it all. She talked about how we came of age at a time of loss: "not loss like a massive destruction, but a loss like something insidious, deep, pervasive."

It is so true, and it is so misunderstood. One of the people commenting on her blog post said, essentially, that it is dangerous to romanticize about a "golden age," that all generations struggle, and that life is hard.

Yes, those things are all true. But they are largely irrelevant to the topic at hand.

There is a very large middle ground between a "golden age" and an "existential struggle." The time and place about which we are both writing (the late 1970s through the present, in the Rust Belt) was neither. But it was undoubtedly a time of extreme transition. It was a great economic unraveling, and we are collectively and individually still trying to figure out how to navigate through it, survive it, and ultimately build something better out of it.

History is cyclical. Regardless of how enamored Americans, in general, may be with the idea, it is not linear. It is neither a long, slow march toward utopia nor toward oblivion. When I look at history, I see times of relative (and it's all relative, this side of paradise) peace, prosperity, and stability, and other times of relative strife, economic upheaval, uncertainty, and instability. We really did move from one of those times to the other, beginning in the 1970s and continuing through the present.

The point that is easy to miss when uttering phrases like "life is hard for every generation" is that none of this discussion about the Rust Belt—where it's been, where it is going—has anything to do with a golden age. But it has everything to do with the fact that this time of transition was an era (like all eras) that meant a lot (good and bad) to the people that lived through it. It helped make them who they are today, and it helped make where they live what it is today.

For those who were kids at the time the great unraveling began (people like me, and people like Della), it is partially about the narrative that we were socialized to believe in at a very young age, and how that narrative went up in a puff of smoke. In 1977, I could smell rubber in the air, and many of my family members and friends' parents worked in rubber factories. In 1982, the last passenger tire was built in Akron. By 1984, 90 percent of those jobs were gone, many of those people had moved out of town, and the whole thing was already a fading memory.

Just as when a person dies, many people reacted with a mixture of silence, embarrassment, and denial. As a kid, especially, you construct your identity based upon the place in which you live. The whole identity that I had built, even as a small child, was of a proud Akronite: This is the RUBBER CAPITAL OF THE WORLD; this is where we make lots and lots of Useful Things for people all over the world; this is where Real Americans Do Real Work; this is where people from Europe, the South, and Appalachia come to make a Better Life for themselves . . .

Well, that all got yanked away. I couldn't believe any of those things anymore, because they were no longer true, and I knew it. I could see it with my own two eyes. Maybe some of them were never true to begin with, but kids can't live a lie the way that adults can. When the mythology of your hometown no longer stands up to scrutiny, it can be jarring and disorienting. It can even be heartbreaking.

We're the middle children of history, man. No purpose or
place. We have no Great War. No Great Depression.
Our great war is a spiritual war. Our great depression is
our lives.

—TYLER DURDEN, *Fight Club*

I'm fond of the above quote. I was even fonder of it when
I was twenty-eight years old. Time, and the realization that
life is short, and that you ultimately have to participate and
do something with it besides analyze it as an outside observer, has lessened its power considerably. It remains the
quintessential Generation X quote, from the quintessential
Generation X movie. It certainly fits in quite well with all of
this. But, then again, maybe it shouldn't.

I use the phrase "Rust Belt Orphan" in the title of this
piece, because that is what the experience of coming of age
at the time of the great economic unraveling feels like at the
gut level. But it's a dangerous and unproductive combination, when coupled with the whole Gen X thing.

In many ways, the Rust Belt is the Generation X of
regions—the place that just doesn't seem to fit in; the place
that most people would just as soon forget about; the
place that would, in fact, just as soon forget about itself;
the place that, if it does dare to acknowledge its own existence
or needs, barely notices the surprised frowns of displeasure
and disdain from those on the outside, because they have already been subsumed by the place's own self-doubt and
self-loathing.

The whole Gen-X-misfit-wandering-in-the-Rust-Belt-
wilderness meme is a palpably prevalent but seldom

acknowledged part of our regional culture. It is probably just as well. It's so easy for the whole smoldering heap of negativity to degenerate into a viscous morass of alienation and anomie. Little good can come from going any farther down that dead-end road.

WHITHER THE FUTURE?

> *The Greek word for "return" is nostos. Algos means "suffering." So nostalgia is the suffering caused by an unappeased yearning to return.*
>
> —"IGNORANCE," MILAN KUNDERA

So where does this all leave us?

First, as a region, I think we have to get serious about making our peace with the past and moving on. We have begun to do this in Akron, and, if the stories and anecdotal evidence are to be believed, we are probably ahead of the region as a whole.

But what does "making our peace" and "moving on" really mean? In many ways, I think our region has been going through a collective period of mourning for the better part of four decades. Nostalgia and angst over what has been lost (some of our identity, prosperity, and national prominence) are part of the grieving process. The best way out is always through.

But we should grieve—not so we can wallow in the experience and refuse to move on, but so we can gain a better understanding of who we are and where we come from. Coming to grips with and acknowledging those things ultimately enables us to help make these places that we love better.

We Americans are generally not all that good at, or comfortable with, mourning or grief. There's a very American idea that grieving is synonymous with "moving on" and (even worse) that "moving on" is synonymous with "getting over it."

We're very comfortable with that neat and tidy, straight, upwardly trending line toward the future (and a more prosperous, progressive, and enlightened future it will always be, world without end, Amen).

We're not so comfortable with that messy and confusing historical cycle of boom-and-bust, of evolution and de-evolution, of creation and destruction and reinvention. But that's the world as we actually experience it, and it's the one that we must live in. It is far from perfect. But for all of its trials and tribulations, the world that we inhabit has one big advantage: it is real.

"Moving on" means refusing to become paralyzed by the past, living up to our present responsibilities, and striving every day to become the type of people who are better able to help others. But "moving on" doesn't mean that we forget about the past, that we pretend that we didn't experience what we did, or that we create an alternate reality to avoid playing the hand that we've actually been dealt.

Second, I don't think we can, or should, "get over" the Rust Belt. The very phrase "get over it" traffics in denial, wishful thinking, and the estrangement of one's self from one's roots. Countless attempts to "get over" the Rust Belt have resulted in the innumerable short-sighted, "get rich quick" economic development projects, and public-private pyramid schemes that many of us have come to find so distasteful, ineffective, and expensive.

We don't have to be (and can't be, even if we want to) something that we are not. But we do have to be the best place that we can be. This might mean that we are a smaller, relatively less prominent place. But it also means that we can be a much better connected, more cohesive, coherent, and equitable place. The only people who can stop us from becoming that place are ourselves.

For a place that has been burned so badly by the vicissitudes of the global economy, big business, and big industry, we always seem to be so quick to put our faith in the Next Big Project, the Next Big Organization, and the Next Big Thing. I'm not sure whether this is the cause of our current economic malaise, or the effect, or both. Whatever it is, we need to stop doing it.

Does this mean that we should never do or dream anything big? No. Absolutely not. But it does mean that we should be prudent and wise, and that we should prefer our economic development and public investment to be hyper-nimble, hyper-scalable, hyper-neighborhood-focused, and ultra-diverse. Fetishizing urban designer Daniel Burnham's famous quote—"Make no little plans, for they have no magic to stir men's blood"—has done us much harm. Sometimes "little plans" are exactly what we need, because they often involve fundamentals, are easier to pull off, and more readily establish trust, inspire hope, and build relationships.

Those of us who came of age during the great economic unraveling and (still painful) transition from the Great American Manufacturing Belt to the Rust Belt might just be in a better position to understand our challenges, and to find the creative solutions required to meet them head-on. Those of us who stuck it out and still live here know where we came from. We're under no illusions about who we are or where we live.

When I look at many of the people of my generation in Akron, I see pragmatism, resilience, self-knowledge, survival skills, and leadership.

He wanted to care, and he could not care. For he had gone away and he could never go back any more. The gates were closed, the sun was gone down, and there was no beauty but the gray beauty of steel that withstands all time. Even the grief he could have borne was left behind in the country of illusion, of youth, of the richness of life, where his winter dreams had flourished.

"Long ago," he said, "long ago, there was something in me, but now that thing is gone. Now that thing is gone, that thing is gone. I cannot cry. I cannot care. That thing will come back no more."

—"WINTER DREAMS," F. SCOTT FITZGERALD

So, let's have our final elegy for the Rust Belt. Then, let's get to work.

CONNOR COYNE

Bathtime

THE BATH DELIGHTS HER.

When it's 6:45 in the evening—dark or getting darker—and we ask her, "You ready to go night-night?" Ruby toddles over toward the stairs, muttering: "Bobble, Eejee." A bottle of milk. Geegee, her stuffed giraffe. She is one year old.

Her eyes light up when we carry her into the bathroom. We drop the plug and press down the plastic mat—you don't want little babies slipping and banging their heads on the hard porcelain—and fill the small room with the silver sound of falling water.

She gives us a big smile as the lukewarm bath surges up around her sides. She laughs brightly when she sees she can make waves by slapping her hands down against the water. She feels buoyed by the bubbles between her toes, the fine mist that catches in her light, pixie hair. She grabs for floating foam letters, a plastic turtle, a rubber duckie. This is one of the happiest moments of her day, and it's good that she is happy before we ask her to keep calm in the darkness, to let her brain slip into sleep, to stop moving for a while. Bath as benediction. A sacred quietness that slips between the

Flinty clatter of distant train wheels rolling. The familiar thrill of train whistles. A reminder of her baptism.

For Ruby, the bath is an immersive experience, and so she tries to dip a plastic cup in the water and take a big gulp. Little kids are immune to parental squeamishness. They do this all over the world, or at least anywhere little kids take baths in porcelain bathtubs. Squeamish parents cringe and say, "No, no, we don't do that. We don't drink water from the tub."

In Flint, though, our reaction is more severe. We lurch forward, our faces pale. It's like catching your toddler tottering at the top of a flight of stairs. It's like seeing a preschooler running headlong toward a busy street in pursuit of a plastic ball. You feel it, visceral in your gut, like someone sucker punched you and you want to puke. They might be making themselves sick from something much worse than suds and whatever scum has been washed away by the day's play.

My wife isn't from Flint.

I am.

Well, I grew up in the city until I was twelve, when my parents moved out to Flushing, a picturesque suburb that finally got its own coffee shop in 1997. That was the year I graduated high school. But even though I had a Flushing address, I auditioned for every play at Flint Youth Theatre and went to the Flint Central High School prom. I always considered myself a Flintstone and spent as much time as I could in the city. When I went away to college in Chicago, I always hoped to come back home. To me, Flint was a place of youthful energy and risk, frisson and connection. I was aware that

I was the salmon swimming upstream, against the current of all the other people eager to leave, but I didn't care.

When I met my eventual wife a few years later, I regaled her with all the stories of my friends and their fucked-up lives. The insane intensity of life in Flint. The city had been abandoned, I said. Physically abandoned by the company that built and nurtured it, and then again by half of its people left struggling in the wake of deindustrialization. Psychically abandoned by a state and nation that had little patience for what they saw as retrograde rust . . . the unrealistic expectations (they thought) of a populace that expected luxury but lacked the ingenuity and the work ethic to hold on to it. Were these assumptions justified? That was one question she might ask. I would shrug. *Occasionally*, I might say. *Usually not.* What was key, though, was that this place broke everyone, and the brokenness made us like Jesus. Conscious suffering, self-aware suffering, opened us up to beatification and grace. We Flintstones cracked open like Easter eggs that offered our provisional yolks as a sacrifice to testify to the flawed construction of the world and its human institutions. Or maybe we were just Buddhas who emptied ourselves inside out so that we could move forward as that best of blank slates: an erased American chalkboard, ready to be filled with knowledge and questions, to offer hope and transcendence to the world at large, and to find peace for ourselves. Inner peace that existed independent of external poverty.

For my wife, practical concerns edged out my visionary rants.

I wanted to go back to the place she said seemed to break everyone I knew (my fault for building the perception, after all, since I told her about the pedo that chased two friends through Woodcroft—the rich neighborhood—in his car, even while my friends in Civic Park and the State Streets— poor neighborhoods—saw neighbors' houses light like jack- o'-lanterns and burn down on a fiery autumn night) . . . how on earth was I going to promise my children a happy, stable childhood in this, my fucked-up home?

"I got this," I said.

I actually felt—and I'm not bullshitting here—more able to deliver that happy, stable childhood in Flint than any- where else. See, in Flint, I knew the rules. It isn't chaos. There are rules. There are especially rules if you're 1) middle-class, 2) white, and 3) educated. And the college education supplied by my father's almost forty years at GM under UAW-earned contracts got me there. My kids would have friends here. They would live in a stable neighborhood and go to a good school. They would have educational opportunities, we'd keep an eye on them, and it wouldn't be any more difficult or risky than a life in Chicago, or New York, or New Orleans, or San Francisco. It would be safer, less risky, because I knew how Flint worked. I didn't know how those other cities worked. I didn't know their rules. I had the tools to control a child's experience of Flint. Anything else, I'd be learning from scratch.

I said this with a lot of arrogance and a fair amount of truth, but hubris always lands the punch line.

When our first daughter was born, we decided to leave Chicago and move to Flint. Because of the fallout from the 2008 housing meltdown, we could afford a house south of Court Street, just east of downtown. When I grew up, this was one of Flint's most exclusive neighborhoods. Now, a family on a single income could land a beautiful 1930s

Tudoresque house for a down payment less than that of the tiniest Chicago bungalow, in the middle range of five figures. We could use the money we saved to choose any school for our daughter we wanted. We were close to my parents. We were close to friends. I planted a garden in our backyard and put up a swing set and a fort. The front yard was filled with dappled sunlight that streamed through the maple leaves each summer, enough shade to cool off, and enough sun to nourish the petunias, iridescent in their violet summer glory.

It was cool.

I knew the rules.

I didn't know the rules.

The rules were bullshit.

I was thinking about classroom sizes and museums and violent crime and copper scrappers. I was thinking about street violence and friends from broken homes and arson and unemployment. Too many guns and too little supervision. These were the problems I was trying to puzzle out. Meanwhile, the city went under state receivership and started drawing water from the Flint River instead of the Great Lakes by way of Detroit. The rest is a sad story told across the world by now: the river water wasn't treated properly; it leached lead and other junk from the pipes into tap water. A lot of people drank that water. A lot of people got very sick. Government officials tried to cover up the catastrophe, leading to more sickness, more delays, more damage.

I had never banked on the water going bad.

In all my youthful exuberance, my desire to bring my girls up here, in my community, my pride, my home, I thought I had covered all of the bases, but water is fundamental, the number-two necessity for humans after breathable air. A place that tries to damage you with its water is damaging in the most basic way. And so, I stayed alert each night, watching Ruby bathe, conscious that this isn't right, that this is supposed to be safe, that she would only be safe, for sure, through our unfailing vigilance.

Ruby doesn't know that the water in this city is bad. Dangerous.

Mary, her five-year-old sister, understands it in a straightforward way, like Darth Vader, like busy traffic, a risk to be avoided. She knows that she shouldn't drink the water just like she shouldn't talk to strangers in strange cars. This loss of innocence and the anonymous lies that prompted it make me sad and angry. Sometimes, it keeps me up at night, thinking of all the injury, the hurt, the real hurt, physical, mental; the loss of trust, the enormity of that loss, the immensity of betrayal; the contempt of those officials who have treated us—treated our children—like expendable animals. Lab rats. Numbers and statistics that might be converted into a political liability, and what a pain in the ass we are for that reason. I've dreamed about it more than once. What if the tests the city conducted on our household water were wrong? What if we didn't act quickly enough? What was this place going to look like in fifteen years? Who was going to be left?

Mary is a bright five-year-old. She is old enough to understand some of this. Not old enough to feel the outrage, but old enough to notice the contradiction and confusion. "It's expensive," we tell her. "Why can't we drink it?" she asks.

"Well," I tell her, "you can wash your hands in it, but don't drink it. Don't you drink it. Even if it's the middle of the night and you're thirsty, come and wake me up. I'll get you a glass. You're right. The world isn't right and the world isn't fair."

Some of these are conversations every father expects to have with his child, but not so soon, and certainly not about the unsafe tap water that costs you $130 each month. Not in the first state to light its darkened city streets with streetlamps. Not in the U.S. state that put the world on wheels and taught it to move with speed.

Ruby isn't even two yet. She doesn't see the confusion or the contradiction. For Ruby, the confusion is much simpler: she likes to dip the plastic cup in her bathwater and take a drink when she can. We freak out, lunge forward, snatch up that cup, and toss it to the floor. Ruby yells in surprise and disappointment, at the loud noise, our worried faces, the brief chaos of moving hands and water spray.

She'll relax again, in a few moments, when we soothe her with a song, or give her something else to play with.

We'll relax, too, when the last of the water has finally vanished down the drain.

Contributors

HUDA AL-MARASHI's essays have appeared in *The Washington Post*, the *Los Angeles Times*, *Al Jazeera*, the *Rumpus*, the *Offing*, and elsewhere. Excerpts from her memoir-in-progress can be found in the anthologies *Love Inshallah: The Secret Love Lives of Muslim American Women*, *Becoming: What Makes a Woman*, and *Beyond Belief: The Secret Lives of Women and Extreme Religion*.

ERIC ANDERSON is the owner of Comics Are Go, a comic book store in Sheffield Village, Ohio, and the author of a collection of poems, *The Parable of the Room Spinning* (Kattywompus Press).

MARTHA BAYNE is a Chicago-based writer and editor whose work has appeared in the *Chicago Reader*, *Buzzfeed*, the *Baffler*, *Belt Magazine*, the *Rumpus*, *Latterly*, and other outlets. She is the editor of *Rust Belt Chicago: An Anthology*, the founder of the Soup & Bread community meal project, and a member of Theater Oobleck's artistic ensemble.

JOHN LLOYD CLAYTON is a writer and teacher in Chicago.

CONNOR COYNE has written two novels—*Shattering Glass* and *Hungry Rats*—and *Atlas,* a collection of short stories, all inspired by the past, present, and future of Flint, Michigan. His website is ConnorCoyne.com and he can be found on Facebook (facebook.com /connorcoyne) and Twitter (@connorcoyne). He lives in Flint with his wife, two daughters, and an adopted rabbit.

G. M. DONLEY is a writer, designer, and photographer. Donley is a longtime resident of Cleveland Heights, Ohio.

SALLY ERRICO is the deputy managing editor at *strategy+business* and the former web manager at *The New Yorker.* Her writing and editing also has appeared in *The New York Times, The Independent,* the *Observer,* the *Rumpus,* and *Northern Ohio Live.* She lives in Brooklyn with her husband and their two children.

DAVID FAULK is a PhD candidate in Germanic studies at the University of Illinois at Chicago. He writes about Arab-German literature of migration and fools himself into thinking that after years of studying Arabic he actually knows the language.

KATHRYN FLINN is a plant ecologist and assistant professor of biology at Baldwin Wallace University in Berea, Ohio. Originally from Indiana, Pennsylvania, she earned a PhD in ecology and evolutionary biology from Cornell.

AARON FOLEY is the author of *How to Live in Detroit Without Being a Jackass* and editor of *The Detroit Neighborhoods Guidebook.* A Detroit native, he worked in journalism for ten years before leading a new neighborhood content site for the City of Detroit, where he currently works.

JIM GRIFFIOEN is a lawyer turned writer and photographer. His work has appeared in *Harper's*, *Vice*, *Time*, *Foam*, *The Baffler*, *Dwell*, and many other publications. He has lived in Detroit since 2006.

BEN GWIN is the author of the novel *Clean Time: The True Story of Ronald Reagan Middleton* (Burrow Press, 2018). His work has appeared in *The Normal School*, *Mary: A Journal of New Writing*, *Belt Magazine*, and others. He lives in Pittsburgh with his daughter.

JEFF Z. KLEIN, born and raised in Buffalo, is a former editor and sportswriter at *The New York Times* and the *Village Voice* and the author of several books about hockey. Currently he writes and produces the "Niagara Frontier Heritage Moments" on WBFO radio. Klein lives in the Allentown section of Buffalo and in Manhattan.

JACQUELINE MARINO is an associate professor of journalism at Kent State University. She is the author of *White Coats: Three Journeys Through an American Medical School* and the co-editor of *Car Bombs to Cookie Tables: The Youngstown Anthology*.

LAYLA MEILLIER is currently graduating from Genesee Early College at the University of Michigan–Flint. She will transfer to New York University to study cinema and begin classes in the fall of 2017.

MARSHA MUSIC is a writer, poet, and self-described "Detroitist," daughter of a pre-Motown record producer; she reflects on Detroit's history and music in numerous books and periodicals, and on her eponymous blog. Ms. Music is a 2012 Kresge Literary Arts Fellow and 2015 Knight Arts Challenge winner, and a noted speaker, narrator, and storyteller featured in Detroit oral histories, podcasts, voiceovers and documentary films.

DAVE NEWMAN is the author of five books, most recently *Please Don't Shoot Anyone Tonight* (Broken River Books, 2017). He lives in Trafford, Pennsylvania, the last town in the Electric Valley, with his wife, the writer Lori Jakiela, and their two children.

JASON SEGEDY is the director of planning and urban development for the City of Akron, Ohio. His passion is creating great places and spaces where residents can live, work, and play.

RYAN SCHNURR is a writer and photographer from northeast Indiana. He is the author of *In the Watershed: A Journey Down the Maumee River.*

AMANDA SHAFFER is a professional coach whose consulting practice serves mission-driven individuals and organizations across higher education and the social sector. Outside of work she is a volunteer with local and national nonprofits dedicated to advancing equity, inclusion, and social progress.

MARGARET SULLIVAN is the media columnist for *The Washington Post.* A native of Lackawanna, New York, she spent most of her career at the *Buffalo News,* where she became the first woman to hold the top editor's position, one she held for thirteen years. She is a former public editor for *The New York Times.*

DR. HENRY LOUIS TAYLOR, JR. is a full professor in the Department of Urban and Regional Planning, as well as the founding director of the Center for Urban Studies at the University at Buffalo. A historian and urban planner, Taylor has authored numerous books, articles, and technical reports on issues relating to the black urban experience and social justice in the United States, Latin America, and the Caribbean. He has received numerous awards for his research and practical activities.

ANNE TRUBEK is the founder and director of Belt Publishing. She is the author of *The History and Uncertain Future of Handwriting* and *A Skeptic's Guide to Writers' Houses*, and the co-editor of *Rust Belt Chic: The Cleveland Anthology*.

CAROLYNE WHELAN is a freelance writer and poet with a special love for the intersection between nature and humanity. Her first book, *The Glossary of Tania Aebi*, was published by Finishing Line Press, and she is currently working on a manuscript about cycling from Canada to Mexico along the Great Divide Mountain Bike Route, listed as one of the hardest cycling routes in the world.

ERIC WOODYARD is an award-winning sports journalist working at MLive.com—The Flint Journal. He is a native of Flint and author of the novel *Wasted*. Woodyard has interviewed many notable celebrities such as LeBron James, Snoop Dogg, Russell Simmons, J. Cole, and Mike Tyson. He appeared on the ESPN's *E:60* and *Outside the Lines* in 2016. Ethan Woodyard is his only child.

Acknowledgments

Thanks to Stephen Morrison for seeing the potential in this book, and Pronoy Sarkar for his enthusiasm and insights.

Thanks to Martha Bayne, who edited the essays that originally appeared in *Belt Magazine*. Thanks to Scott Atkinson, who edited *Happy Anyway: The Flint Anthology*; Eric Boyd, editor of *The Pittsburgh Anthology*; Anna Clark, editor of *A Detroit Anthology*; Jody Kleinberg Biehl, editor of *Right Here, Right Now: The Buffalo Anthology*; Jacqueline Marino and Will Miller, editors of *Car Bombs to Cookie Tables: The Youngstown Anthology*; Jason Segedy, editor of *The Akron Anthology*; and Richey Piiparinen, co-editor of *Rust Belt Chic: The Cleveland Anthology*.

Neither *Belt Magazine* nor Belt Publishing would have been able to originally publish these essays without Nicole Boose, William Rickman, Karie Kirkpatrick, Michelle Blankenship, Meredith Pangrace, David Wilson, Aaron Foley, Anna Clark, Haley Stone, Matt Stansberry, Michael Jauchen, Jim Babcock, and the many generous members of Belt.